Dr. Lee Ann B. Marino, Ph.D., D.Min., D.D.

AN EVOLUTION OF LOVE IN THE
BIBLE (AND WHAT IT MEANS
FOR US)

Created For Love

Created For Love
AN EVOLUTION OF LOVE IN THE BIBLE
(AND WHAT IT MEANS FOR US)

Dr. Lee Ann B. Marino, Ph.D., D.Min., D.D.

Published by:
Remnant Words
(*An imprint of the Righteous Pen Publications Group*)
www.righteouspenpublications.com

All rights reserved. Except as permitted under the U.S. Copyright Act of 1976, no part of this book may be reproduced, distributed, or transmitted in any form or by any means, electronic or mechanical, or saved in any information storage and retrieval system without written permission from the author.

Unless otherwise noted, Scripture taken from **The Holy Bible, New Living Translation** copyright © 1996, 2004, 2007 by the Tyndale House Foundation. Used by permission of Tyndale House Publishers, Inc., Carol Stream, Illinois 60188. All rights reserved.

All Scripture quotations marked KJV are taken from the **Holy Bible, Authorized King James Version,** Public Domain.

Book classification: Books > Religion & Spirituality > Christian Books & Bibles > Bible Study & Reference > Language Studies

Cover and interior photos are in the Public Domain.

Copyright © 2019, 2025 by Lee Ann B. Marino

ISBN: 1-940197-59-7
13-Digit: 978-1-940197-59-3

Printed in the United States of America.

*With Your unfailing love
You lead the people
You have redeemed.
In Your might,
You guide them
to Your sacred home.
(Exodus 15:13)*

Table Of Contents

	Acknowledgements.............................	i
	Introduction: Love in the Bible................	1
1	*Attraction ('Ahab and Eros)*....................	17
2	*Familial Alliance (Storgay)*.....................	55
3	*Deliberate Affection (Hesed)*...................	101
4	*Friendship (Raham and Phileo)*................	131
5	*Divine Love (Agape)*...........................	165
	Conclusion: Connected by Love................	193
	References..	197
	About the Author...............................	199

Acknowledgements

I sincerely thank those who have loved me, those that I have come to love, and all I have learned about love from – both the good and the bad through the years – as I strive to gain a more balanced and detailed perspective on the work of love in our natural and spiritual lives. Thank you for inspiring the need for this book!

Introduction

LOVE IN THE BIBLE

IT'S a many splendored thing. It's exciting and new. I thought it wasn't meant to last. It's the inspiration for hundreds of thousands of songs. It's the thing everyone hopes to find at least once in their lives. It goes through phases, it goes through changes, and in the long run of humanity, it feels like none of us really knows just what it is. It's become a conundrum, something we aspire to yet don't understand, and overuse it all the time. From fuzzy little puppies to our favorite television show...we claim to recognize it in fairy tales and think we understand it best within ourselves.

It's love. Ah, love. Don't we all love, love? Well, don't we?

OK, maybe not. Maybe it's better to say that we love what we think love is. We like the idea that love is whatever fairy tale notion we've concocted, whatever idea that we've formulated, whatever perception of it that we'd like to think we will receive from others. We want to receive it, we want to feel it in our lives, and we want to have it all to ourselves. We just don't want to give it to others or discipline ourselves to the realities that love requires.

That's right: love requires something of us. Maybe that's why we are so elusive when it comes to really understanding love. We'd much rather adopt the ideal concepts of love that we thought existed in fairy tales and emotional stories that filled us with awe and wonder in relationships. The idea that all we need to do to find love and balance exists in surrounding ourselves with perfect people might sound like an interesting challenge in the beginning, but it won't take long for it to feel like a hopeless feat, something that has absolutely no shot at ever happening. As we get older, we realize we can't control others, we can't change others, and it easily can feel like loving other people (let alone finding love for ourselves) is something largely unobtainable.

Love can seem like an impossible feat, no matter what our belief system might be. The world today seems cruel, heartless, and there are all too many people who never find love personally. Then we hear stories of those who thought they found love, only to lose it later on. It seems the world is washed in selfishness, abuse, hate, and unkindness, and the more we go on, the more it seems like love lacks everywhere. Yet something somewhere inside of us still pushes us on to find it, even though it doesn't seem obtainable. We look for it in other people, we seek satisfaction from our work and from things that will never have the ability to love us back, we look for love in all the wrong places, still believing it is out there, somewhere...even though it seems elusive.

Does love exist? Can we find it? When we do, what will it look like? To answer these questions, we need to look no further than the Scriptures.

Why is love in the Bible?

Surely in this day and age you have probably heard one of the many complaints raised about Christianity. People who claim to be Christians are hypocrites (well yes, some are). Preachers are just in ministry for money (well yes, there are some who are). Christians have terrible marriages (well yes, this can be true). Christians are mean (definitely have met a few of those in my day). Christians don't act like Jesus (also have seen this one). Most Christians respond to these statements with a sense of indignation. They are offended that people are so quick to judge all Christians for what they perceive a few to do and often explain away the question or issue raised by saying that you can't judge everyone by what a few do. They are then often quick to label those who don't seem to follow the rudimentary aspects of Christian faith as "religious," while they are in some way not "religious," but "spiritual" or "in a relationship with God." They claim to have the answer or solution, but what is often said isn't very different from that which others have to offer.

Dr. Lee Ann B. Marino, Ph.D., D.Min., D.D.

The thing that is often hardest to swallow about people who respond to these issues in such a way is the mere fact that they often behave the same way those "other" people do. They might have some clever or quick answers for whatever they think as far as how a Christian life should be lived, but it tends to fall into buzzwords. They still fall back on the same claims, the same issues, and the same problems. It seems like they are still trying to get others to do all the same things: go to church, attend a special event (such as a conference or revival), and do exactly what everyone else does in the process. Whenever someone expresses a differing opinion or is in somehow "different" from others, that is almost always a cause for a verbal assault, a lecture, or alienation from the general community.

What I am about to say might shock you: the arguments that people make against Christians are often correct. The only notable objection I might make to such arguments is that they tend to be generalizations, which means even though they might apply to more than a few Christians, they don't apply to everyone. There are plenty of Christians who seek to live out their faith, day in and day out, to the best of their ability. Yet even I can't deny that there are plenty of people who claim to be Christian, who might even seem to have some semblance of Christianity in the exterior points of their lives, who just don't live up to the title of "Christian."

There are a few reasons why I believe this is, especially in our modern times. The first is that I don't think enough is expected of the average believer. Most churches give the thorough impression that one is all right with God if they maintain their financial and social status at the church while avoiding certain behaviors or actions that are clearly deemed "unacceptable." Most church leaders avoid dealing with sinfulness or improprieties that the "average person" commits, while focusing on whatever issues are deemed to be "big sins." We also have a sort of American independent disconnect going on today that emphasizes personal relationship without the balance of church and community. When people go off on their own in their faith without structure, accountability and community support, the result becomes a faith that is void of much power. Instead of focusing on the things they need to transform in themselves, they start focusing on everyone and everything else in the hopes that their problems aren't so severe they miss out on God.

The way we have insulated ourselves to avoid dealing with our own issues and private demons is the very reason why love is mentioned in the Scriptures, time and time again. The problem with such avoidance is that it does cause us to miss out on God, but that's not the only thing it causes us to miss out on. It causes us to miss out on the amazing and incredible connection that He has designed us to have with one another. The entirety of the Scriptures is about connection: how disconnected we entered this life to begin with, the consequences of disconnection, and all that God has done to restore connection within our lives. That is why we hear about love in the Scriptures: to get our attention and prove to us that the right relationship can change our lives. It's not a relationship with a man or a woman or someone who is non-binary or restoring our relationships with our parents or family that will do it, however. It is a right relationship with God through Christ, one that alerts us to our need for change and the impact and empowerment of overcoming things in our lives. God has already reached out through Christ, and now the rest of the answer is up to us. Whether or not we desire to work with God unto the end of transforming everything within our lives is up to us.

The Scriptures exist as a record of humanity's interaction with God Himself. We learn through the Bible that love is a Being...love is God, Himself. By learning about the different ways God has interacted with humanity and studying, believing, and standing through the challenges of Scripture that don't always make sense to us, we are able to come to a place where we have experienced a written record of God's love, and we can see it in a certain sense through life. It may not always be easy to understand, and we might have points where we stumble or fail to see things clearly at first, but we can always stand with that written record and remember exactly Who God is and what He is doing for us, today, too.

So, if this incredible revelation of love is foundational to the Christian experience, why do Christians seem to have such a hard time manifesting the results of such a life-changing experience themselves, in their own lives and their own perspectives? There are many reasons why it might be, but there is another question that many raise in response to such issues. If Christians don't seem to be able to get this right, is the answer in finding something else?

Are other religions the answer?

I just acknowledged the overwhelming failure of the Christian community to live different in this world. I am acknowledging that because I believe love acknowledges and tells the truth. Whether you are a Christian or not, I can't write this book and pretend that Christians know everything there is to know about love, because we don't. Too many of us haven't taken the time to delve into the Scriptures enough to come to a revelation about love and just trusting what someone else tells them has led many acclaimed believers to believe they love when they, in actuality, are not displaying love in their lives, at all. We have created a viscous battle between love, principle, and following God, making all three antithetical to one another. Because people have seen, grown up in, or experienced generation after generation of Christians who just don't measure up, we are now living with the results. People assume Christianity isn't real, nor is it what it claims to be, and are looking for alternatives in other religions. After all, maybe there is an answer somewhere else, right? Buddhists seem peaceful. Hindus seem devout. Muslims seem committed to the cause. Jews seem devoted to their lineage. New Agers claim to love everybody. Is love prevalent in another religious system? Can one learn more about love somewhere else?

It's an interesting question but I think the answer lies in the very heart of the questions addressed about the systems themselves. The first reality is while the grass might seem greener somewhere else, all religious systems have problems and issues because all religious systems contain people. There is always someone, somewhere, who doesn't embody or espouse the views that a group claims to have. In the west, we pay careful attention to the hypocrisies of Christians because various Christian denominations are our immediate exposure. In other countries, however, you hear stories about other groups in the same context. In Muslim countries you hear stories about hypocrites in Islam, in Hindu nations you hear stories about hypocrites in Hinduism, in Buddhist nations you hear stories about Buddhist hypocrites, in Jewish nations you hear stories about Jewish hypocrites. Even the New Age Movement, with its mash-up of belief systems, has numerous stories of people who just don't measure up to its ideals, no matter how noble they might seem on the surface. No matter where you go in the world and no matter how much the glittering appeal of another religion might sparkle and shine, the disappointments of human nature will find you.

The second reality is the centrality of love is not a theme in other religious systems as it is in Christianity. Buddhism focuses on enlightenment, Hinduism focuses on ritual, Islam focuses on submission to the will of

Allah, Judaism focuses on study and knowledge of one's system, and the New Age Movement is focused on a coming perfect era of history that has not yet come. While other religious groups are highly structured, many of their adherents may be highly devout, they may be very disciplined, and it may appear that their adherents are all on the same page, the reality of such is that none of these things equate to a true sense of love in one's life. There are many people who grew up in non-Christian religious systems who felt isolated, lonely, even alienated from others, no matter how devout they might have been in practice. They might have done great things, they might have been sincere and noble, and they might have even believed in what they stood for or did, but that doesn't mean they did what they did with a sense of love. Love may be mentioned from time to time in other systems, but that doesn't make it a focus. As a side point love might be a nice idea, it might be something that stands as a side point but isn't the prominent aspiration of a group. If it's not a focus, if it's not something that changes and touches everyone, then it won't be something that one develops in a profound way.

The third reality is that while yes, human nature can be a terrible and distorting thing, that doesn't mean everyone in Christianity has abandoned love and its foundational relevance to faith. Christians don't get it all right, but that's what makes God that much more incredible, maybe in a strange and backward-sounding way. No matter what we do, no matter who we are, no matter what we believe, God still loves us and wants the very best for each and every one of us. It is only through the revelation of the Scriptures and the teaching of a true Christian heart that we can hear of a deity that espouses this kind of true love and true faith for His people. Other gods expect and demand, but Christians can say that they have experienced God Who loves them – not because of what they have done, but despite whatever it might be. This doesn't mean that everything we do is pleasing in God's eyes, but it does mean that there is nothing that can take us away from the profound sense of love and relationship that God always desires with us.

So yeah, Christians don't always measure up; but neither does anyone else. This is not stated to excuse Christian behavior or misrepresentation, but it is to help us realize that there isn't anything better somewhere else. Coming to know God and the love of God transforms and changes our entire lives, and while everyone else might not measure up, we all know we can step up and experience something great with God if we are willing to walk the road with Him.

Created for relationship

Why should we learn about love? My best guess is that if you've picked up this book, it's probably because you are interested in learning more about it. Whether you are seeking love in a greater way for yourself or you want to learn more about loving others and giving love, learning about love is something we all want to explore at some point in our lives. We should learn about love because it is part of both human and spiritual experience. The word "love" is thrown around an awful lot, but for a word that is used frequently, we don't often define it or seek to expound upon it. That means if we don't know what the word means, we can use it improperly or incorrectly, and such can leave us confused as to its meaning. It doesn't help that people often tell us they "love" us and then don't, causing further confusion as to just what love is.

The confusion about love is the enemy (Satan's) way of confounding us about it, making sure we are thoroughly uncertain of where to look for it and how to recognize it. The world we live in is marred by sin or deliberately seeking to alienate itself from God. Sin has created a divide, one by which a lot of things that should make sense don't, and the result of that confusion is separation. It is thanks to sin that human nature is so complicated, crazy, unfathomable, and sometimes alienating and evil. God is not the reason that we sin; we are. As we follow the leading of things that aren't of God, we fall into patterns, behaviors, temptations, decisions, and choices that take us away from His will and into things that cause both ourselves and others trouble. Sin is the opposite of love; it is the opposite of the good nature of God.

Sin is complicated because God has created us for relationship, thus making such an innate, inborn desire within all human beings. The complication comes in because sin makes our desire for connection and relationship with others distorted. Those different patterns, behaviors, temptations, decisions, and choices cloud our concepts of what love should be and of our ability to love others. This means that we may walk through our lives with difficulty connecting to other people for any number of reasons: we might have trouble communicating, we might pick all the wrong people to be around us as intimate friends and lovers, we might gravitate toward certain destructive habits, or we might isolate. We might do none of these things but do other things that are just as destructive. Our negative behavior and those of others often isolates and makes it difficult to connect, and at some point in time we will seek out answers or ways to heal the damaged parts of us that seem to make sense. Some of those different answers and methods might work some of the time, but over time, something will feel like it's missing. The old habits might come back or might be replaced with new ones. Trying to do this on our own doesn't work. That is where God and His infinite love step in.

We can't do this "love thing" on our own without God. To learn about love and embrace love for ourselves we must first embrace God and set ourselves to get right with Him. It is a lifetime commitment. You won't do it all perfectly. Yet in this initial, life-building experience that we have with God gives us the ability to interact differently with others. As we let God into our lives, we let God's love change who we are, and we move from a place of confused and jumbled-up alienation to connection. This leads us to want better connections, purposes, and relationships with others, all built on the extension of this great love that we now have.

The catch is we can't give what we don't have, and we can't do what we don't understand. While people talk a lot about "love" in the Bible, there are at least five different terms that we translate as "love" into English. These different expressions cover an entire spectrum of human experience: attraction, familial alliance, deliberate kindness, friendship, and finally divine love, that which changes us for the better. Through these different forms and expressions of love we learn a lot about human interaction and about how to touch every aspect of our lives with a sense of God's presence. In this little book, we are going to take a look at the different forms of love that are present in the Scriptures: *'Ahab* and *eros*, *storgay*, *hesed*, *raham* and *phileo*, and *agape*. Delving into all these words we describe in English as "love" and their meanings will set us afire and aflame with an empowered understanding, drawing us to a better idea of the connections God desires for His people as we interact with Him and with one another. Here we will learn how to embrace what we have through Him, give what we have received, and offer what we now understand.

A few notes on our study

When you aim to study different forms of the word "love" in the Bible, scholars and commentators usually expound on four different Greek terms that are translated as the word "love" into English. These four different words are *eros*, *storgay*, *phileo*, and *agape*. There's nothing wrong with these studies; I have done them myself in a couple of my older books. The thing I found when studying for this book is that we are eliminating Hebrew terms for "love," which are just as revealing and important to our study of love as the Greek words. In fact, some of those Greek terms have Hebrew parallels which further expound and encompass the understanding of the ways those words are used.

Some chapters of this book will feature two words instead of just one – A Hebrew word and a Greek word. These words are paired together because the meanings of the two words are, for the most part, parallel in meaning. Sometimes their extended definitions may vary, but for the basic understanding of the word, they are alike enough to comment on and explore their meanings together.

In every chapter, I will first post the definition of the words we will be exploring, in their entirety. The reason for this is simple: ancient languages were often simpler than those we employ today, and for that reason some words have multiple definitions. If we want to understand the fullness of what is expressed through these words, we need to see what they mean, fully and completely.

As we walk through the definitions of the words, we will explore their meaning beyond their definitions. We will look at insightful truths and principles God desires us to learn and embrace as we walk through the complex world of love this side of heaven. It is my goal that we will see progression in our study of love: that certain types and explorations of human interaction lead us to an open door for other types of love and human exploration in our lives. Our ultimate goal is to come to a place where we experience and express divine love. We learn shadows and pieces as we study other forms, and it is God's desire that as we grow through and seek greater in our lives, we shall find it.

It is also my hope that as you read and study with this little book you will recognize and see yourself in different places: both where you are doing great, and where you can grow in improvement. When it comes to love, no believer is completely there or where they need to be. Carrying around our issues that have related to sin – not just our own, but the consequences of those sinful actions of others – makes it so our concept of love is jaded and complex, and we are continually walking out our spiritual call to love greater, deeper, and more powerfully in this life.

So here we shall begin our crash course on love – one that we will find ourselves face and confront time and time again as we experience the meeting of new people, new issues, new ideas, and new challenges – throughout our lives. Sometimes touching, sometimes funny, and always new and exciting, let's learn about what God has to say to all of us about love (and why it is so vitally important).

Chapter One

○────────♡────────○

ATTRACTION (*'AHAB* AND *EROS*)

'Ahab[1]

אֲהָבִים 'ahab {aw-hab'} or אָהֵב 'aheb {aw-habe'}

Meanings:
- to love
- human love for another, includes family, and sexual
- human appetite for objects such as food, drink, sleep, wisdom, human love for or to God
- act of being a friend
- lover (participle)
- friend (participle)
- God's love toward man, to individual men, to people Israel, to righteousness
- lovely (participle)
- loveable (participle)
- friends
- lovers (fig. of adulterers)
- to like

> **Eros**[2,3]
> ἔρως {ehr-os}
> **Meanings:**
> - To desire
> - love
> - sexual passion

THE first example of love that we find in the Scriptures is that of 'ahab in the Hebrew. Though it is used in many different ways throughout the Old Testament, it is first used to describe Abraham's relationship with Isaac in Genesis 22:2. It goes on to describe a host of marital relationships, attractions, and relationship interests throughout the Old Testament, including God's relationship with Israel. As the first form of love in the Bible, you'd figure that it is simple and uncomplicated, but that is far from the truth. It may be one of the most complicated forms of love out there – and that means as our first encounter or draw with love, it sets the stage for us to encounter and conceptualize love throughout our lives.

In this chapter we will be looking at humanity's first encounter with love: 'ahab in Hebrew, and *eros* in Greek. Both terms refer to a very similar experience, and here in English, we define it as "love." In some ways, however, we could probably translate it a little differently and understand it a little bit better, a little bit clearer, and understand just what it is referring to so we understand it in our lives. In some ways it is a very challenged and controversial form of love, and due to its complexities, it can be easily maligned in English. It is also ironic that it is often the most challenged form of love, for various reasons. So many experience it...but never understand it...and here we seek to understand it as a launch for growth and perspective in all areas of love in our lives.

Properly defining 'ahab and eros in English

I stated in the introduction that ancient language wasn't quite as clearly defined as language is today. What this means is that in times past, words weren't often as specific in their meanings as they are now. One word could be used to describe any number of different meanings, all understood within their context and usage. This is one of the reasons why Bible translation is such a challenge for people who undertake the work: translators have the challenge of interpreting words based on how they were used back in their day, now in the context of an array of word choices that have different and more evolved meanings. It might not sound like a big deal on the surface, but the truth is that making those kinds of language choices is a complicated aspect of interpretation. It doesn't help that we have certain understanding and implied traditions when it comes to interpretation that keeps words translated in certain ways (archaic by modern standards) even though the usage and understanding of such words is different today. Believing that translations done hundreds of years ago are somehow superior to what we can understand in language today is part of what keeps our translations – and our words – in standard concepts that people don't ever break out of, or see the difference in their understanding and meanings.

The few Biblical renderings of words we translate as "love" don't all equate to the same kind of experience with love. The terms *'ahab* and *eros* are such an example. Both are quite different in form than the Greek word *agape*, but because of the primitive nature of the languages, they may overlap in relationships where it might seem another kind of love is required. This is all because language is complicated, people are complicated, relationships are complicated, and the way that any person might feel, interact, or regard someone or something else can be extremely complicated. Thus, older words in older languages reflect these complications. They reflect just how difficult love, interest, and attraction to someone or something might be, and just as the feelings we have for someone or something might overlap, so, too, do ancient words.

'Ahab describes an entire expanse of experience in love: love between people (whether familial or sexual in nature); human interests, appetites, and desires; friendship; lovers; God's love toward humanity, Israel, and the right thing; something deemed as lovely or desirable; and like.

The Greek word *eros* defines its intents a little more simply, desire, love, or sexual passion. The term *eros* is not found in the Hebrew Bible but is alluded to in the Septuagint (or Greek translation of the Old

Testament), especially in the Song of Solomon. In these two terms, we find something common rooted in their definitions, often translated simply as love: we find a root of attractiveness and desire, seeking something out because there is something in it that draws us to it.

Thus, we could say that *'ahab* and *eros* are an attraction or desire for something else, and just what that thing is that draws us can vary. Whatever the thing or reason for the drawing is, it causes us to hold a certain affection and interest for it, and the results of that are an impulse, a split-second desire to connect with whatever that might be for the immediate or throughout our lives. *'Ahab* and *eros* teach us a lot about ourselves: what we like most, what we seek most, what turns our heads and charms us, and what we desire. For this reason, I often define *'ahab* and *eros* as attraction.

Our first examples of "attraction"

One would probably assume the term *'ahab* to be used in connection with Adam and Eve in the Bible. We know he was surprised to see her, from how we read the text we can recognize he was taken with her, and we know they had their own children, which indicates the two of them had a sexual relationship. Yet it's surprising to note that there is no Hebrew term for "love" anywhere in the story of Adam and Eve. No term exists to describe any human interaction or relationship in those generations between Adam and Abraham, at all. We see many examples of forming familial responsibility and duty, but we don't see the kind of loving connection we might expect to exist among families today. Why is this? Shouldn't there be some sort of loving example in these relationships?

It's probably safe to say that people might have been interested in or attracted to one another in all sorts of contexts before Abraham's time, but there wasn't a description or understanding of it on a large scale. Remember, these were records of very primitive people on earth, and people might not have thought about defining their relationships at that point in time. People probably were interested in each other, they had certain connections to one another, but they hadn't lived long enough to try and define things. They were sorting it all out as they had experiences, and coming to have those continual experiences helped them to start to figure out there was more involved in their relationships than just mere mechanics.

The other reason we probably don't see much love in the first twenty-two chapters of the Bible is because people didn't regard relationships back then in quite the same way that we do today. We will talk more about this in the next chapter, but the realities of life and marriage are that the purpose in marriage and the attitude about love and families wasn't quite so emotional or romantic back then. As the first people on earth, their experiences of survival and living often took precedence over personal feelings and interest. The evolution of the term for love, associated with being drawn to something, shows us progress in human history from mere survival to making decisions, choices, and recognizing certain forms of like and interest. They were choosing between different things – desiring some and rejecting others as less desirable – and that also represents a knowledge of self, of tastes and interests, and desiring to pursue those in life. Humanity was moving past surviving harsh winters and conditions and starting to think about how one felt about another. Way to go, humanity!

Our first instance of love in the Bible describes the relationship between Abraham and Isaac.

SOME TIME LATER, GOD TESTED ABRAHAM'S FAITH. "ABRAHAM!" GOD CALLED.

"YES," HE REPLIED. "HERE I AM."

"TAKE YOUR SON, YOUR ONLY SON—YES, ISAAC, WHOM YOU LOVE SO MUCH—AND GO TO THE LAND OF MORIAH. GO AND SACRIFICE HIM AS A BURNT OFFERING ON ONE OF THE MOUNTAINS, WHICH I WILL SHOW YOU." (Genesis 22:1-2)

This first instance of "love" in the Bible is used because it illustrates a drawing, or an interest, between two different things by implication. Abraham had two sons, Ishmael and Isaac. Ishmael was the firstborn son, born because of his relationship with Sarah's slave, Hagar. From what we read in the Scriptures, the relationship between Abraham and Hagar was a particular issue between Abraham and Sarah, and such converted to issues between

Sarah, Ishmael, and later Isaac in their lives. There was constant conflict and tumult, and the family, consisting of one man, a wife, a concubine, and two resulting children was a complete and total mess. We know that when things became particularly arduous, Abraham sent Hagar and Isaac away in what appears to be a departure for the rest of their lives. This means that when faced with the choice of his two children, Abraham chose Isaac over Ishmael. Isaac was the child God promised he would have, he was his appointed and future heir, and while his lineage would rest with both sons, Abraham saw more of a future and a promise through Isaac.

In other words, Abraham was drawn to Isaac over Ishmael. The relationship with Isaac was more desirable, more attractive. He didn't feel about Ishmael in the same way he felt about Isaac, and Abraham picked between the two. I've heard it described in many ways, but I would probably say that Abraham found himself very taken with Isaac. He reflected Abraham's life and desire for an heir in a different, more complete way than Isaac did, and that means he favored Isaac, he desired the best for Isaac, and he wanted to spend his time and attention on Isaac. Isaac was Abraham's choice, his appeal, and his attraction. It wasn't in a sexual sense, but it was very much in the sense that someone wants something over something else and decides they will pursue it.

That's why Abraham and Isaac are our first instance of love in the Scriptures. Abraham made a choice between two different people and chose one over another. This is a central aspect to our intimate relationships of all sorts today. Whenever we choose a friend, a husband or wife, a mate, an acquaintance, or a family member that we're just closer to than the rest, we are experiencing a principle of attraction in that something draws or connects us to one person over another. In other words: we love, with a strong affection, that which attracts, interests, or draws us. Our first impulse to affection is always going to be that which is easiest to love, and in the instance of *'ahab* and *eros*, we see the power of loving that which engages us in some way.

Once we see the use of love in Abraham's relationship to Isaac, we start seeing it throughout the Old Testament. The Scriptures go on to use the same terminology for love to describe other human relationships: between Isaac and Rebekah, between Jacob and Rachel, and so on and so forth, to describe over 209 different encounters and relationships in the Old Testament. They encompass the entirety of human experiences and even begin to touch the heart of the divine and our relationship with God. In Old Testament love, we experience an introduction to everything: to human relationships, to choices and interactions that we make in our relationships, to our pursuit of divine things and our pursuit of anything that is our personal choice and desire. What this teaches us in a powerful way is the relevance of deciding to pursue relationships and putting forth effort to make them work, because they are something we choose.

Dr. Lee Ann B. Marino, Ph.D., D.Min., D.D.

Created for one another

I've often heard it said to lonely people that even though they might not have friends, a serious relationship, or family around them, that they "still have God," and that having God "is enough." There are many reasons why I take objection to saying such to someone who is lonely. The first is that it isn't a very loving thing to say. It sounds like you don't care about them or how they are feeling, and that you are brushing off loneliness as if it's not a relevant or important thing. Such a statement, while it might sound comforting theologically, sounds isolating in reality. The reason for this is actually quite simple: God did not just create us to "have God." He did not exclusively call us into relationship with Himself, but with others, as well. No human person is an island, and that means our relationships with others bespeak a lot about our relationship with God, as well as about us, as people.

Old Testament love is all about these intricate relationships that are often complicated, intense, indescribable, and require a great deal of effort to maintain. God created humanity with eternity in mind, and for our walk both in this life and in the next, we will be called to handle the challenges and purposes of relationships with one another. That's why when we talk about love, it has so many components to it. The story of love is the story of human interaction. It's about love, hate, war, peace, conflict, satisfaction, dissatisfaction, attraction, intimacy, ideas, concepts, affection, anger, frustration, alienation, and beyond. The entire expanse of human experience is wrapped up in the concepts about love and the fight to overcome alienation.

This is why I believe understanding a concept of attraction or drawing together is why humanity first recognized love at play and in purpose. God has placed a desire in every human being with the expressed intent and anticipation to overcome the isolation we all feel. Our entire life struggle is about overcoming the alienation we experience as human beings. To understand why we experience this alienation, we must understand that little three-letter word that causes us so much trouble in our lives – sin.

In the Hebrew, the word "sin" literally means "to miss the mark." To understand this properly, we need to think of the concept of a bullseye in archery. Those who practice with the bow and arrow seek to hit the middle of the target, because that's where the most points are found. This type of skill was important in developing one's ability to hit a target, because in ancient times, the goal of such "target practice" wasn't to play a game for sport, but to prepare for hunting. If you couldn't hit the target right where it was needed, it could mean the difference between a long-standing meal for your community or starvation. It's important to be accurate, to get things right, and to operate as efficiently as possible.

The catch with such target shooting is no matter how much you practice, it becomes inevitable that you will, at times, miss the target. Despite your best efforts, your greatest desire to hit that target every time, you won't do it. This is kind of like what sin is like. No matter how much we try, we just don't get it right of our own power, all the time. When we sin, we miss the mark with God. We hit around, we hit off to the side, or we might hit something else all together, but we don't find ourselves moving, aiming, and operating exactly where we should be. This results in a loss, because it means we find ourselves outside of the will of God.

Thus, if we understand sin properly, sin separates because it doesn't keep us where we should be. It causes division from God as well as division from others. In sin, we seek a certain sense of independence that drives us and wants our own way, no matter what kind of hurt or harm it might cause. Over time, most of us come to a place where we understand that sin is alienating and hurtful, not just to others, but to us, as well. In love, we seek to break through that alienation caused by sin. We want to be with other people, we want to love and be loved, and we want to experience something that draws us out of ourselves and away from the results of our own stubborn will and independence.

The catch is that we often try to seek out this loving interaction through the eyes of sin. We can desire relationships with others based on concepts or for all the wrong reasons. That's what makes our struggle against isolation so difficult. We can think we are seeking a good thing, but if we don't center God in our lives, we will always find ourselves looking for love in difficult places. We know we are created for more than being alone, but we have to be willing to put in the time to learn and explore love for things to turn out in a better way.

Throughout history people have found themselves in a lot of trouble as they strive to be loved by the wrong people, in wrong situations, or in circumstances where love becomes manipulative and crazy. We can see examples of such in the Old Testament, which are provided for us to recognize it's something that we have all done.

THEN DELILAH POUTED, "HOW CAN YOU TELL ME, 'I LOVE YOU,' WHEN YOU DON'T SHARE YOUR SECRETS WITH ME? YOU'VE MADE FUN OF ME THREE TIMES NOW, AND YOU STILL HAVEN'T TOLD ME WHAT MAKES YOU SO STRONG!" SHE TORMENTED HIM WITH HER NAGGING DAY AFTER DAY UNTIL HE WAS SICK TO DEATH OF IT. (Judges 16:15-16)

IN THE MEANTIME, SAUL'S DAUGHTER MICHAL HAD FALLEN IN LOVE WITH DAVID, AND SAUL WAS DELIGHTED WHEN HE HEARD ABOUT IT. (1 Samuel 18:20)

NOW KING SOLOMON LOVED MANY FOREIGN WOMEN. BESIDES PHARAOH'S DAUGHTER, HE MARRIED WOMEN FROM MOAB, AMMON, EDOM, SIDON, AND FROM AMONG THE HITTITES. THE LORD HAD CLEARLY INSTRUCTED THE PEOPLE OF ISRAEL, "YOU MUST NOT MARRY THEM, BECAUSE THEY WILL TURN YOUR HEARTS TO THEIR GODS." YET SOLOMON INSISTED ON LOVING THEM ANYWAY. HE HAD 700 WIVES OF ROYAL BIRTH AND 300 CONCUBINES. AND IN FACT, THEY DID TURN HIS HEART AWAY FROM THE LORD. (1

Kings 11:1-3)

MY CLOSE FRIENDS DETEST ME.
THOSE I LOVED HAVE TURNED AGAINST ME.
(Job 19:19)

IF YOU LOVE SLEEP, YOU WILL END IN POVERTY.
KEEP YOUR EYES OPEN, AND THERE WILL BE PLENTY TO EAT! (Proverbs 20:13)

"THEN OHOLAH LUSTED AFTER OTHER LOVERS INSTEAD OF ME, AND SHE GAVE HER LOVE TO THE ASSYRIAN OFFICERS. THEY WERE ALL ATTRACTIVE YOUNG MEN, CAPTAINS AND COMMANDERS DRESSED IN HANDSOME BLUE, CHARIOTEERS DRIVING THEIR HORSES. AND SO SHE PROSTITUTED HERSELF WITH THE MOST DESIRABLE MEN OF ASSYRIA, WORSHIPING THEIR IDOLS AND DEFILING HERSELF. FOR WHEN SHE LEFT EGYPT, SHE DID NOT LEAVE HER SPIRIT OF PROSTITUTION BEHIND. SHE WAS STILL AS LEWD AS IN HER YOUTH, WHEN THE EGYPTIANS SLEPT WITH HER, FONDLED HER BREASTS, AND USED HER AS A PROSTITUTE.

"AND SO I HANDED HER OVER TO HER ASSYRIAN LOVERS, WHOM SHE DESIRED SO MUCH. THEY STRIPPED HER, TOOK AWAY HER CHILDREN AS THEIR SLAVES, AND THEN KILLED HER. AFTER SHE RECEIVED HER PUNISHMENT, HER REPUTATION WAS KNOWN TO EVERY WOMAN IN THE LAND. (Ezekiel 23:5-10)

All these situations have one thing in common: they involved what we might call a "fatal attraction." They were situations where seeking someone (or something) out led to the destruction of someone or something. Delilah used Samson's feelings to manipulate him. Michal never found what she sought through David, and their relationship did not have a fulfilling end. Solomon's pursuit of pagan women led to his downfall as leader of Israel. Job's pursuit of his friends in a difficult time led to their turn against him. If you only seek after sleep, you will never find yourself able to work. Oholah lusted after individuals to the point where she prostituted herself as a pagan temple prostitute, thus resulting in a life pursuit with such individuals that ended badly. These examples prove to us that what – and who – we love in our lives is very important, and not everything that turns our head leads to a godly end. If we are seeking out relationships or ideas of things with the haunts of sin in our lives: hurt, emotional wounds or pain, or try to seek from a relationship or thing what we can only find in God, we will always come up short. We are created for one another, and that means we must attune ourselves to examine what draws or attracts us and make sure those pursuits have God at the beginning and end of them.

Not every example of love in the Old Testament cautions us in our relationships. There are also examples of great love between people that transformed and changed entire situations.

AFTER DAVID HAD FINISHED TALKING WITH SAUL, HE MET JONATHAN, THE KING'S SON. THERE WAS AN IMMEDIATE BOND BETWEEN THEM, FOR JONATHAN LOVED DAVID. FROM THAT DAY ON SAUL KEPT DAVID WITH HIM AND

WOULDN'T LET HIM RETURN HOME. AND JONATHAN MADE A SOLEMN PACT WITH DAVID, BECAUSE HE LOVED HIM AS HE LOVED HIMSELF. JONATHAN SEALED THE PACT BY TAKING OFF HIS ROBE AND GIVING IT TO DAVID, TOGETHER WITH HIS TUNIC, SWORD, BOW, AND BELT. (1 Samuel 18:1-4)

KISS ME AND KISS ME AGAIN,
FOR YOUR LOVE IS SWEETER THAN WINE.
HOW PLEASING IS YOUR FRAGRANCE;
YOUR NAME IS LIKE THE SPREADING FRAGRANCE OF SCENTED OILS.
NO WONDER ALL THE YOUNG WOMEN LOVE YOU!
TAKE ME WITH YOU; COME, LET'S RUN!
THE KING HAS BROUGHT ME INTO HIS BEDROOM. (Song of Solomon 1:2-4)

THEN THE LORD SAID TO ME, "GO AND LOVE YOUR WIFE AGAIN, EVEN THOUGH SHE COMMITS ADULTERY WITH ANOTHER LOVER. THIS WILL ILLUSTRATE THAT THE LORD STILL LOVES ISRAEL, EVEN THOUGH THE PEOPLE HAVE TURNED TO OTHER GODS AND LOVE TO WORSHIP THEM." (Hosea 3:1)

The love of the Old Testament is both human and divine, but its understanding is far more human than divine. God reached out to all of us on a level we could understand, and in the Old Testament, we recognize this level to reflect the seeking, searching, and overcoming of human nature to try and love, in both distorted and wholesome ways. Our interactions, both with God and with others, are ever perfect. Giving a true record of the human condition, the Old Testament reveals to us just how difficult it is to live with others, work toward overcoming sin, and still strive to love and be loved in this unfair world.

Let's talk about sex, baby

Now we segue into some of the more challenging aspects of Old Testament love and attraction, and it is those that relate to physical interest, attraction, and sexual expression. Challenging or not, these are a part of the *'ahab* and *eros* world of love present in the Old Testament, and we need to rise to recognize what God desires to teach us about such relationships for ourselves.

In the 1990s the group Salt n' Pepa mastered the charts with their hit song, *Let's Talk About Sex*. The song itself was a rallying cry for women to discuss their relationship downfalls and dissatisfactions with their partners, especially their male partners. The song was vitally important because it was the first time that a popular pop song called out the difficulty in discussing sex and love in a relationship. Even all these years later, people still struggle to talk about such issues with intimate partners and in a general sense, with others. Among church crowds we get particularly intimidated by the idea of discussing sex as a part of loving relationships. It's not part of all loving relationships, but we can't deny that a heavy part of the Old Testament Hebrew and Greek words for love bear with them a sexual implication or understanding. Not all relationships were sexual, and not all relationships were chaste, either, and understanding that love can mean and manifest in more than one way is a big part of our personal growth in perspectives of love.

The sexual connotation of *'ahab* and *eros* are both very well defined, but the front-and-center love of *eros* is found prominently in the Song of Solomon. Most people openly admit to never studying the Song of Solomon, let alone pulling apart its racy content for us to discuss and examine from a spiritual perspective. Even though we, as people, think sex is dirty, God does not agree with us, and when done as a part of a truly loving and committed relationship, sex is a part of God's plan for us. It is one of the ways that we are able to express different thoughts, feelings, and emotions to another person, but the catch is that we can't come to recognize this if we don't ever talk about the issue to begin with.

The Song of Solomon is important considering love and sex because there is no love without sex in this specific, specified, intimate relationship example. The book is believed to be a wedding song between two people who were preparing for their entire lives together. This tells us that such intense, sexual connection is often part of marriage relationships, no matter who the people in that relationship may be. Even though we are quick to joke about sex in marriage as if it is an oddity, a sexual relationship is what most desire in such a relationship. If you are married and sex is not part of it (for reasons other than those related to orientation, health or physical inability), that means it's time to examine that relationship and why that is. If there is some reason why you aren't connecting with your marital partner in that way, there is probably a deeper reason. Sometimes people argue the issue of loving someone but not being in love with them, and whether one wants to accept that as an answer, examinations into Biblical love do raise the reality that it is possible to love someone as a person but not be attracted to them in a sexual sense. Since love is complicated, there can be many ways different combinations of love and attraction overlap, and the reality is that this happens in marriage just as much as it happens anywhere else.

We won't be talking a whole lot about this here, however, because it is more of our purpose to focus on the relevance of human sexuality in our lives, as an expression of love and commitment. We all know people can have sex without commitment or love, and we also can see the consequences of such. Whenever we try to divorce intimate connection from any sort of love or intimacy, the result can be increased feelings of isolation. Remember, one of our major goals in this life is a desire to connect with others. When we are always in situations that create a façade of closeness, but soon after lead to disconnection, we are going to feel lonelier and alone and less connected.

The Song of Solomon shows us that sex can be a powerful form of connection between people, and connection is a part of love. The couple in the Song of Solomon didn't just hop into bed and start their sexual relationship.

The powerful imagery present in the book shows they moved into their sexual intimacies because of their intense attraction and desire for one another. They took their time and learned about each other, which drove them to desire each other, even more.

THE KING IS LYING ON HIS COUCH,
    ENCHANTED BY THE FRAGRANCE OF MY PERFUME.
MY LOVER IS LIKE A SACHET OF MYRRH
    LYING BETWEEN MY BREASTS.
HE IS LIKE A BOUQUET OF SWEET HENNA BLOSSOMS
    FROM THE VINEYARDS OF EN-GEDI.

YOUNG MAN
HOW BEAUTIFUL YOU ARE, MY DARLING,
    HOW BEAUTIFUL!
    YOUR EYES ARE LIKE DOVES.

YOUNG WOMAN
YOU ARE SO HANDSOME, MY LOVE,
    PLEASING BEYOND WORDS!
THE SOFT GRASS IS OUR BED;
FRAGRANT CEDAR BRANCHES ARE THE BEAMS OF OUR HOUSE,
    AND PLEASANT SMELLING FIRS ARE THE RAFTERS.
(Song of Solomon 1:12-17)

LIKE THE FINEST APPLE TREE IN THE ORCHARD
    IS MY LOVER AMONG OTHER YOUNG MEN.
I SIT IN HIS DELIGHTFUL SHADE
    AND TASTE HIS DELICIOUS FRUIT.
HE ESCORTS ME TO THE BANQUET HALL;
    IT'S OBVIOUS HOW MUCH HE LOVES ME.

STRENGTHEN ME WITH RAISIN CAKES,
   REFRESH ME WITH APPLES,
   FOR I AM WEAK WITH LOVE.
HIS LEFT ARM IS UNDER MY HEAD,
   AND HIS RIGHT ARM EMBRACES ME.
PROMISE ME, O WOMEN OF JERUSALEM,
   BY THE GAZELLES AND WILD DEER,
   NOT TO AWAKEN LOVE UNTIL THE TIME IS
RIGHT. (Song of Solomon 2:3-7)

MY LOVER SAID TO ME,
   "RISE UP, MY DARLING!
   COME AWAY WITH ME, MY FAIR ONE!
LOOK, THE WINTER IS PAST,
   AND THE RAINS ARE OVER AND GONE.
THE FLOWERS ARE SPRINGING UP,
   THE SEASON OF SINGING BIRDS HAS COME,
   AND THE COOING OF TURTLEDOVES FILLS THE
AIR.
THE FIG TREES ARE FORMING YOUNG FRUIT,
   AND THE FRAGRANT GRAPEVINES ARE
BLOSSOMING.
RISE UP, MY DARLING!
   COME AWAY WITH ME, MY FAIR ONE!" (Song of
Solomon 2:10-13)

ONE NIGHT AS I LAY IN BED, I YEARNED FOR MY
LOVER.
   I YEARNED FOR HIM, BUT HE DID NOT COME.
SO I SAID TO MYSELF, "I WILL GET UP AND ROAM
THE CITY,
   SEARCHING IN ALL ITS STREETS AND SQUARES.
I WILL SEARCH FOR THE ONE I LOVE."
   SO I SEARCHED EVERYWHERE BUT DID NOT
FIND HIM.
THE WATCHMEN STOPPED ME AS THEY MADE
THEIR ROUNDS,

AND I ASKED, "HAVE YOU SEEN THE ONE I LOVE?"
THEN SCARCELY HAD I LEFT THEM
 WHEN I FOUND MY LOVE!
I CAUGHT AND HELD HIM TIGHTLY,
 THEN I BROUGHT HIM TO MY MOTHER'S HOUSE,
 INTO MY MOTHER'S BED, WHERE I HAD BEEN CONCEIVED. (Song of Solomon 3:1-4)

The most important line of these verses is found in 2:7: don't awaken love until the time is right. When it comes to love, marriage, and sex, we are often quick to jump the gun and keep up with the person next to us. It makes us feel inferior to watch our friends and acquaintances get married or find successful relationships, only to stand back and realize we don't have one. This can make us think there is something wrong with us and drive us all the more to settle for relationships that lose their fizzle or don't withstand the complications and trials of married life. Love as relates to intimacy in marriage comes when the time is right for any and all who desire it. Not everyone seeks it out, but many do, and when we find it, we know it.

In other words, when we are in a relationship that brings together a godly sense of sexuality along with an intense attraction and connection, we will know that the right love is there by spiritual instinct. This is what makes our intimate relations different than just bed hopping or just trying to make a relationship work without God. God's emphasis on love in relation to sexuality is simply because we do need God in our relationships to make them successful and lasting. God's key to this is godly communication, one between partners that emphasizes honesty, discussion of preference, like and dislike, and a sense of openness between one another. If a relationship doesn't have this, it will lack sexual intimacy as well as a general sense of connection and oneness.

In intimate relationships, we should find a sense of unity, of oneness, something that brings us back to our Creator and Originator in a spiritual sense. This doesn't mean that intimate partners are the same or come to a place where they ignore one another's differences. It means that we recognize God has brought us to our partner, and we celebrate the image of God present within them as well as the presence of God in our relationship. Our union with our mate should bring us to a place where we recognize our relationship with God is more important, more essential, and closer than this moment, because it involves the eternal and Almighty God.

We also can learn from marital love because our spiritual relationship with God is compared to a marriage. There are many reasons for this, but one of the most poignant is because it gives us an idea we can relate to in covenant. We will speak more about this in an upcoming section, but it is worth mentioning here. God wants us to understand what He desires for and with us, nothing more, and nothing less. While we are not the same with God as we might be with our spouse, it is a pretty good illustration for us about the intensity with which God loves each one of us.

Appreciating and celebrating creation's form

Do you understand the difference between love and lust? Do you think every time you find another human being attractive, you are guilty of lust? I think one of the reasons why we are often confused about love is because we confuse love and lust. We assume that any time we find someone or something attractive or interesting, that means we must love them. It is perfectly possible to think someone, or something is attractive and not be in love with them, but for intimate relationships to begin, there must be a foundational point where attraction or desire is involved.

In Old Testament times, the division between "like" and "love" wasn't so clearly defined. In the New Testament understanding of love, the two are very, very different. We will explore this more in a later chapter and understand it for ourselves. The truth is that such is an understanding we grow into, however, and that if we don't understand this, it's easy to think that everyone who was attracted or drawn to someone or something loved it. The Scriptures aren't an entire biography of any Biblical figure's life, and that means we have the most important details instead of the day-to-day journal of their actions. We don't know about all the women Isaac liked but didn't desire to pursue, or all the Israelite women who turned Solomon's head, or all the temptations Abraham faced in Egypt. Naturally, not everyone loved everything they saw, but they certainly had times where they looked and saw beauty or precision in form with appreciation.

Old Testament love is about what draws us, and that means anything that draws us, both in a general and more specified sense. It carries with it a special association of sexual love or interest and often speaks of impulsive or spontaneous attraction. This means that Old Testament relationships were seen as a bigger part of an entire picture, and any and all attraction and resulting affection could fall under its larger heading. It also clarifies for us that there is nothing wrong with realizing a certain sense of beauty and promise in the human body.

THEN GOD SAID, "LET US MAKE HUMAN BEINGS IN OUR IMAGE, TO BE LIKE US. THEY WILL REIGN OVER THE FISH IN THE SEA, THE BIRDS IN THE SKY, THE LIVESTOCK, ALL THE WILD ANIMALS ON THE EARTH, AND THE SMALL ANIMALS THAT SCURRY ALONG THE GROUND."

SO GOD CREATED HUMAN BEINGS IN HIS OWN IMAGE.
IN THE IMAGE OF GOD HE CREATED THEM; MALE AND FEMALE HE CREATED THEM.

THEN GOD BLESSED THEM AND SAID, "BE FRUITFUL AND MULTIPLY. FILL THE EARTH AND GOVERN IT. REIGN OVER THE FISH IN THE SEA, THE BIRDS IN THE SKY, AND ALL THE ANIMALS THAT SCURRY ALONG THE GROUND." (Genesis 1:26-28)

The Scriptures tell us the human being is created in the image, or likeness, of God. This doesn't mean that we are literally God, but that God has created us and endowed us with certain characteristics that are a part of His own being. This means that while God Himself does not have a body, being in a human body is not shameful because we are all created within the image of God. That means when we appreciate human form – finding such attractive, appealing, or beautiful – we are appreciating a part of God's creation. Such can be a prominent sign of respect and of honor to God in an indirect way, because it shows admiration for God's creation.

This also means that love and admiration can be to things as well as to people; it can be toward anything in creation. We can love nature, we can love our pets or animals, we can love the beauty that we see around us in creation, and we can have a special and healthy respect for our planet and our ecosystems because we respect the Creator's hand in their existence and function. It's not just about loving people, but any love and any attraction toward or to anything.

When we understand love in an Old Testament sense, it encompasses a sense of spontaneous, instant attraction, something that is recognized in someone else. The question remains, who is the sense of "love" for in this instance? Is it for the person, for what they see, or for the Creator behind it? The answer can be all three, or one or the other. Whenever we appreciate what God has created, it is a silent, instant way that we offer a certain level of honor and praise to the One Who created it. By seeing the work of God, we have a spontaneous, impulsive draw to God through His work.

Of course, there are instances where this is not the case, and the admiration goes beyond that of the Creator to the creature, which we shall talk about next. Still, what we can find in instant attraction and appreciation of human form is simple: it is something that is given by God in order to help keep things functioning down here, as well as connecting us to Him, in a way we have often never expected.

Attraction vs. lust

One of the reasons we avoid discussion of attraction (especially in spiritual principle) is because people think attraction equates to the same thing as lust. This isn't true, and the two are not the same. The reason people associate the two is because they can have much in common, with the major difference being the direction of admiration. One results in a worship of God while the other results in the worship of oneself or of something or someone else. Sometimes situations warrant all definitions, sometimes one or the other, but what this teaches us is that love can be abstract, because we can be drawn to loveliness as a principle, present in a thing, rather than in a person.

Lust is an attraction that is distorted. It involves the same principle as attraction, but views something without a sense of love behind it. It puts the person or thing on a plane above God, above everything else in one's life, to the detriment of the individual(s) involved. Simply put, lust is idolatry in its drawing form. Before it becomes a full-fledged idol, it is an object that one desires and must have separated from its Creator. It might not be something that one pursues full-time, but its purpose is just strong enough to compromise it spiritually.

Much of the time when we talk about idolatry we talk about it in the case of loving something more than we love God. This is an appropriate definition, but I think it can be misleading to us because it sounds like our love of God is about our feelings rather than our behavior. It also makes people think that chasing idols is all about chasing obvious, visible concepts of a false deity, as one sits around and bows down to a statue or something as they abandon worship of God. As one who has been in ministry for over twenty years as of the writing of this, be assured that I have met plenty of people who were led into idolatry by various intense lusts, and they all came to church every Sunday, hands in the air, singing all the songs, and living in disobedience behind the scenes. There were many reasons why it happened and came to where it was at: they were lonely, their ambitions outshined practical reason and purpose, they didn't have enough life experience to avoid the temptations, etc., but in the end, their pursuit of whatever it was lured them away from their love of God. Whether it was recognized as such, or not, it was there and was a pervasive part of their being until they were willing to handle and deal with whatever it was that was keeping them from God. Loving God – love in the Bible – is almost always a verb, rather than a noun.

That means whenever we love something more than we love God, we are doing something to put it before God – and obedience to Him – in our lives.

IF YOU LISTEN TO THESE REGULATIONS AND FAITHFULLY OBEY THEM, THE LORD YOUR GOD WILL KEEP HIS COVENANT OF UNFAILING LOVE WITH YOU, AS HE PROMISED WITH AN OATH TO YOUR ANCESTORS. (Deuteronomy 7:12)

AND NOW, ISRAEL, WHAT DOES THE LORD YOUR GOD REQUIRE OF YOU? HE REQUIRES ONLY THAT YOU FEAR THE LORD YOUR GOD, AND LIVE IN A WAY THAT PLEASES HIM, AND LOVE HIM AND SERVE HIM WITH ALL YOUR HEART AND SOUL. (Deuteronomy 10:12)

BE CAREFUL TO OBEY ALL THESE COMMANDS I AM GIVING YOU. SHOW LOVE TO THE LORD YOUR GOD BY WALKING IN HIS WAYS AND HOLDING TIGHTLY TO HIM. (Deuteronomy 11:22)

DO NOT FALL INTO THE TRAP OF FOLLOWING THEIR CUSTOMS AND WORSHIPING THEIR GODS. DO NOT INQUIRE ABOUT THEIR GODS, SAYING, 'HOW DO THESE NATIONS WORSHIP THEIR GODS? I WANT TO FOLLOW THEIR EXAMPLE.' (Deuteronomy 12:30)

YOU MUST NOT TURN AWAY FROM ANY OF THE COMMANDS I AM GIVING YOU TODAY, NOR FOLLOW AFTER OTHER GODS AND WORSHIP THEM. (Deuteronomy 28:14)

SO BE VERY CAREFUL TO LOVE THE LORD YOUR GOD. (Joshua 23:11)

BUT YOU THOUGHT YOUR FAME AND BEAUTY WERE YOUR OWN. SO YOU GAVE YOURSELF AS A PROSTITUTE TO EVERY MAN WHO CAME ALONG. YOUR BEAUTY WAS THEIRS FOR THE ASKING. YOU USED THE LOVELY THINGS I GAVE YOU TO MAKE SHRINES FOR IDOLS, WHERE YOU PLAYED THE PROSTITUTE. UNBELIEVABLE! HOW COULD SUCH A THING EVER HAPPEN? YOU TOOK THE VERY JEWELS AND GOLD AND SILVER ORNAMENTS I HAD GIVEN YOU AND MADE STATUES OF MEN AND WORSHIPED THEM. THIS IS ADULTERY AGAINST ME! YOU USED THE BEAUTIFULLY EMBROIDERED CLOTHES I GAVE YOU TO DRESS YOUR IDOLS. THEN YOU USED MY SPECIAL OIL AND MY INCENSE TO WORSHIP THEM. IMAGINE IT! YOU SET BEFORE THEM AS A SACRIFICE THE CHOICE FLOUR, OLIVE OIL, AND HONEY I HAD GIVEN YOU, SAYS THE SOVEREIGN LORD. (Ezekiel 16:15-19)

There were a million reasons (or so it would seem) why the Israelites kept falling into their idolatrous ways, over and over again, in the Scriptures: they wanted to be like their neighbors, they wanted to fit in with others, they wanted to get the results they all had, they wanted to do what they did. The base of that problem, however, was lust. They were driven by their desires, their lusts that contrasted with their relationship with God. It was more important to them to have what they sought than to obey God and trust Him for all their needs.

Isn't this much how idolatry starts in all of us? Sure, we might think we are above it, but what draws us is what we pursue, and we pursue what we love. Idolatry reveals a disconnect in our heart and our results, between what we claim to love most and best, and what we really love best, in our reality. Love of God means we must distance ourselves from people and things that seek to take us away from Him. If we recognize God as our source of love, we cannot seek out things contrary to Him and still say we love Him before all else.

God and His people

In the Old Testament, we learn that God called the Hebrew people out from their nations, religions, and cultures of origin to become the nation of Israel. In Bible times, the people of Israel had a long and complicated relationship with God. It seems like every time we turn around, we find long and involved stories detailing Israel's failures before God. God selected these people for His own, He made a covenant with them, or a long-standing agreement, affirming their relationship. Both God and Israel had responsibility in that agreement. God selected and loved Israel, choosing them not because they were the largest or greatest of all nations, but because they were a small, intimate group that could know Him and reap His benefits in a personal way. It was God's responsibility to care for them and to bring the Messiah to and through them. It was Israel's job to follow God's statutes, showing their love and care for Him as a unique people. They were not to be strayed off into the ways of their pagan neighbors, they were not to follow the ways of other gods, they were not to worship those false gods, and they were to honor one another in a way that others did not. By nature of their covenant, God married Israel. They were His unique people, and He loved them. They were to love Him, too, but somehow, that often got confused and muddled in the translation.

This doesn't change God's love for His people, however. Because His first covenant with Israel didn't turn out well, God established a new covenant, this time with anyone who would come to Him sincerely for salvation. We are now God's people, we are now "married" to God. The form of love that God describes in His relationship with Israel is as a marriage, comparing Himself to a husband and Israel, as His wife or bride. We also see this imagery present between Christ and the church in the New Testament.

FOR YOUR CREATOR WILL BE YOUR HUSBAND; THE LORD OF HEAVEN'S ARMIES IS HIS NAME! HE IS YOUR REDEEMER, THE HOLY ONE OF ISRAEL, THE GOD OF ALL THE EARTH. (Isaiah 54:5)

BUT YOU HAVE BEEN UNFAITHFUL TO ME, YOU PEOPLE OF ISRAEL! YOU HAVE BEEN LIKE A FAITHLESS WIFE WHO LEAVES HER HUSBAND. I, THE LORD, HAVE SPOKEN. (Jeremiah 3:20)

WHEN THE LORD FIRST BEGAN SPEAKING TO ISRAEL THROUGH HOSEA, HE SAID TO HIM, "GO AND MARRY A PROSTITUTE, SO THAT SOME OF HER CHILDREN WILL BE CONCEIVED IN PROSTITUTION. THIS WILL ILLUSTRATE HOW ISRAEL HAS ACTED LIKE A PROSTITUTE BY TURNING AGAINST THE LORD AND WORSHIPING OTHER GODS." (Hosea

1:2)

FOR WIVES, THIS MEANS SUBMIT TO YOUR HUSBANDS AS TO THE LORD. FOR A HUSBAND IS THE HEAD OF HIS WIFE AS CHRIST IS THE HEAD OF THE CHURCH. HE IS THE SAVIOR OF HIS BODY, THE CHURCH. AS THE CHURCH SUBMITS TO CHRIST, SO YOU WIVES SHOULD SUBMIT TO YOUR HUSBANDS IN EVERYTHING.

FOR HUSBANDS, THIS MEANS LOVE YOUR WIVES, JUST AS CHRIST LOVED THE CHURCH. HE GAVE UP HIS LIFE FOR HER TO MAKE HER HOLY AND CLEAN, WASHED BY THE CLEANSING OF GOD'S WORD. HE DID THIS TO PRESENT HER TO HIMSELF AS A GLORIOUS CHURCH WITHOUT A SPOT OR WRINKLE OR ANY OTHER BLEMISH. INSTEAD, SHE WILL BE HOLY AND WITHOUT FAULT. IN THE SAME WAY, HUSBANDS OUGHT TO LOVE THEIR WIVES AS THEY LOVE THEIR OWN BODIES. FOR A MAN WHO LOVES HIS WIFE ACTUALLY SHOWS LOVE FOR HIMSELF. NO ONE HATES HIS OWN BODY BUT FEEDS AND CARES FOR IT, JUST AS CHRIST CARES FOR THE CHURCH. AND WE ARE MEMBERS OF HIS BODY.

AS THE SCRIPTURES SAY, "A MAN LEAVES HIS FATHER AND MOTHER AND IS JOINED TO HIS WIFE, AND THE TWO ARE UNITED INTO ONE." THIS IS A GREAT MYSTERY, BUT IT IS AN ILLUSTRATION OF THE WAY CHRIST AND THE CHURCH ARE ONE. SO AGAIN I SAY, EACH MAN MUST LOVE HIS WIFE AS HE LOVES HIMSELF, AND THE WIFE MUST RESPECT HER HUSBAND. (Ephesians 5:22-33)

Some question the appropriateness of speaking of God as a husband to His people, because people imply something sexual in the connotation. As I spoke on it earlier, the sexual relationship between spouses doesn't mean we are sexually intimate with God but represents a oneness and a closeness we should strive to have with Him. As we look over these different Scriptural passages, we learn that God's relationship with His people (first with Israel, and now with us) is one of a truly committed, intimate relationship that is meant not just to be life-long, but eternal in nature. It also means that we learn a lot about love by viewing God's relationship with His people.

- **Love makes an agreement** – In the case of Israel, God kept meeting His end of the agreement, but Israel kept failing to keep theirs. In love, we make our agreements, and we keep them. We don't expect the other person to do it all. Our contribution to our relationship might be different, but it is important we bring something to the table, something that we can offer in the process.

- **Love sacrifices** – Love gives of itself. This doesn't mean a relationship should be where one is consistently giving, and one is consistently receiving, but that when we truly love others, we are willing to give something of ourselves to the relationship.

- **Love is a unity** – Love brings people

together. Because love is from God, it connects us to one another, and to Him, as well.

- **Love teaches us about God** – Love shows us a shadow, or a likeness, of what God is all about. Because we are human, it doesn't show it perfectly, but it does give us an idea of what God's love for us is like when we are willing to love others.

- **Love is commitment** – Whether we are making a commitment to a marriage, to raise a child, to raise a puppy, or to keep a house plant alive, we are agreeing to do our part to make something work in the long-term. It won't work if we don't have love behind us, because love is what drives us to do what needs to be done, day after day, even when we are tired and no longer feel as if we want to pursue whatever it is we have undertaken.

The love we experience this side of heaven is here to remind us of our relationship with God. It is to point us to that time when we no longer experience or battle sin in this world. It's not always perfect and not always expressed as we might like, but the good, powerful experiences we have with love remind us of our Creator. They also help us to embody His characteristics in our lives, especially when life becomes difficult or tedious.

Bearing all in love

The attraction and desire factor in Old Testament love shows us that when we are drawn into things – whether good or bad – we find ourselves in a place of vulnerability. This results when we let down all the walls of sin that keep us bound and become transparent and real, exposing a side of us we don't let the whole world see, because love gives us the ability to feel safe, comfortable, and instill trust within us.

This is where the relevance of God in our spiritual lives transforms and merits change within us. There is no love present if there is no transparency, no vulnerability to break through the problems and issues that we have. We can't get better if we are unwilling to admit we have a problem. Whether we have a specific problem, a general issue with sin, or an overall need to get over ourselves (or maybe all three), we need to be willing to bare ourselves in a revealing sense to receive God's love that will transform our lives.

WILL BE GLAD AND REJOICE IN YOUR UNFAILING LOVE, FOR YOU HAVE SEEN MY TROUBLES, AND YOU CARE ABOUT THE ANGUISH OF MY SOUL. (Psalm 31:7)

LONG AGO THE LORD SAID TO ISRAEL: "I HAVE LOVED YOU, MY PEOPLE, WITH AN EVERLASTING LOVE. WITH UNFAILING LOVE I HAVE DRAWN YOU TO MYSELF. (Jeremiah 31:3)

No matter how bad things are with others, we need to always remember that God does love us. It's not a substitute for the things people do or for the ways we might feel put off or mistreated by others, but it is a greater love, a greater awareness. Just like we are drawn to any assortment of things, God is drawn to us. He desires we know Him and that we engage with Him in knowledge and relationship. We can always trust that when we are honest and transparent with God, He won't misuse or abuse it. In being that way, we can come to a place of discovery and true healing, being people of change. The entanglements of sin confine us, but love liberates us. Whenever we tap into love, we are tapping into God. Whenever we are hurt by what we thought was love but was not, the answer to overcome is still love. Love is honesty; love is truth; and in all things, true love is God.

Reflections

- Why are the Old Testament words for love so broad and general?

- Why is attraction and desire so central in Old Testament definitions of love?

- Why is marital love used as an illustration of love between God and His people?

- What can you learn from your own desires and attractions about your own love walk?

Chapter Two

FAMILIAL ALLIANCE (*STORGAY*)

Philostorgos[1]
φιλόστοργοι philostorgos {fil-os'-tor-gos}

Meanings:
- the mutual love of parents and children and wives and husbands
- loving affection, prone to love, loving tenderly
- chiefly of the reciprocal tenderness of parents and children

Storgay[2]
στοργή storge {stor-gay}

Meanings:
- Cherishing one's kindred, especially parents or children
- fond of natural relatives, i.e., fraternal
- toward fellow Christians
- kindly affectioned

Dr. Lee Ann B. Marino, Ph.D., D.Min., D.D.

THE Old Testament terminology for words often translated as "love" in the English encompassed an entire expanse of definitions: everything from attraction to sex to parents and children to friends and family members, and beyond. We learned from Old Testament love just how complicated love is, how many things it can encompass, and how we can be drawn to good things and good people or bad things and bad people, all as part of human experience. Now as we start to look at more specified definitions of things related to love, we recognize that there are different kinds of love and ways that love manifest in our lives.

In this chapter we are going to specifically look at the influence of *storgay*, which directly relates to love and affection in families and those who are close enough to be considered family. While it's not a word that is directly found in the Bible, a variation of it does exist, and there are many different examples of its principles and concepts in Bible text. Even though we often take for granted that love should exist in families, we know well enough it often does not, and what we often don't consider is how it operates (and why), in the first place. Learning about familial love gives us a heads up on our relationship within the church, and how we can repair our own issues by learning more about essential love that stands as our first teacher for loving other people.

Properly defining storgay (and its derivatives)

Storgay is typically defined as a love for one's

family members, specifically natural relatives. By extension, it can also relate to those we think of as family, friends or close associates who might not be blood relatives. It is exclusive in this context, as it is not used to define a love for things other than family, not for things or people other than those we are very close to. It also does not define our relationship with God in any sense, so it is limited in its understanding. This makes it easy for us to visualize, as well as identify.

To properly understand this word, I define it as familial alliance. It hits at the very heart of the survival of a group or clan. In order for a group to exist and continue to thrive, there must be some sort of group identity that unites and bonds them together. This is the very foundation of *storgay* and of its uniting force between families: survival. By seeing their unique commonalities, they recognized and saw the need to stay together, and the result were the bonds formed of day in, and day out emphasis to work together for mutual survival.

In the New Testament we find the word *philostorgos*, which is a derivative of the root *storgay*. This particular term describes a mutual love existing between family members, a certain bond that mixes a concept of love among friends with love among family members. It is like *storgay* amped up, expressing and defining that relationship rather than just saying it is vaguely about connections between family members. It defines this bond is to be based in love, and we also learn it is the bond of love that is to exist among those who are a part of Christ's church. Thus, in church, we are to have a loving alliance, one that unites us together and forms a common bond in Christ.

Our first encounters with love

Studies have proven that our idea of love and how it is defined most often comes from our early familial experiences. Outside of this general consensus, no one quite specifically agrees how those ideas are formed within us or how they change as we mature and enter into society independent of our families. This is not to say that our ideas and concepts about love and loving relationships can't change or can't be influenced elsewhere, but it is to say that a lot of how we view the world and how much we trust other people has its origins in how we are treated as children and how our family interacts within the familial unit. What this tells us is that our early histories give us concepts and ideas about how our interactions with others are supposed to work.

This isn't to say that we are completely and totally doomed if we didn't have perfect childhoods. It is just to recognize that early on in our lives, the people who claim to love us are the people who give us an idea of what that word – love – is supposed to mean. It's for this reason that Genesis – which means "beginnings" – is all about relationships, especially among family members of one sort or another. In each foundational relationship we have we experience certain ideas about how things should (or sometimes shouldn't) be, and those impact the way we might feel about pursuing those relationships later on in our lives. It's not an accident that much of the familial stories in Genesis are decidedly dysfunctional, rather than idealistic: they give us all the message that familial relationships are complicated, and while survival might have been foremost for all involved, it doesn't mean people didn't get sidetracked one in awhile with something or some idea or concept about relationships to overcome later.

UNLESS THE LORD BUILDS A HOUSE,
   THE WORK OF THE BUILDERS IS WASTED.
UNLESS THE LORD PROTECTS A CITY,
   GUARDING IT WITH SENTRIES WILL DO NO GOOD.
IT IS USELESS FOR YOU TO WORK SO HARD
   FROM EARLY MORNING UNTIL LATE AT NIGHT,
ANXIOUSLY WORKING FOR FOOD TO EAT;
   FOR GOD GIVES REST TO HIS LOVED ONES.

CHILDREN ARE A GIFT FROM THE LORD;
   THEY ARE A REWARD FROM HIM.
CHILDREN BORN TO A YOUNG MAN
   ARE LIKE ARROWS IN A WARRIOR'S HANDS.

HOW JOYFUL IS THE MAN WHOSE QUIVER IS FULL OF THEM!
   HE WILL NOT BE PUT TO SHAME WHEN HE CONFRONTS HIS ACCUSERS AT THE CITY GATES.
(Psalm 127:1-5)

I think it is most important to note that familial love is very much a concept based in survival. It emerged to define the alliances and relationships that families have with each other. The thing we need to realize is that this type, or form, of love wasn't always fuzzy and warm like we understand it to be today. It's very possible that someone might regard a familial duty as necessary without having a lot of warm, fuzzy emotions surrounding it. It was strictly about duty, honor, and responsibility among one's own kind, making sure that the lineage of a group continued from generation to generation. A family couldn't be fed, survive harsh weather conditions, protect itself from invading groups or clans, fight disease, and ever see a day where their own kind would propagate and continue the family line without some sort of agreement and alliance to work together toward that common goal.

Storgay explains why people keep returning to their families of origin, even when they reject or outright disown them. It explains why abused children always seem to want their abusive parents, even when love is not found in that relationship. It explains why no matter how many people love you unconditionally, it is so hard to break that desire and want for families of origin. It's a concept and an expectation that an alliance and familial "bond," of sorts, should be there, just by virtue of the fact that people are related. When this doesn't happen it is confusing, because it is against our basic instincts of survival.

Storgay can also be complicated because familial love often sounds great and sounds idealistic, but the reality behind it is if it is not developed and tempered properly it can be highly exclusionary. I've met more than a few people who believe their only obligation as

Christians or people in general is to love their families, and no one else. They create an "us vs. them" mentality, pitting the family against the whole world. Familial alliance (familial love) is an extension of how we love ourselves and those who are most like us, and relishes in separateness from others: what makes us "us," unique, different, and separate from other people. In summary, we can say it is about identification. Yet if we leave ourselves in such a position to avoid interacting with others, we can easily believe the only love to be achieved in this lifetime is with family.

Loving what looks like us

If you've been in church over the past twenty or so years, you probably have heard a lot about family. In fact, some churches go as far to label themselves as "family worship centers" or "family churches" in the hope of attracting a specific type of family: parents with young children. Complete with youth ministry and children's church, one looking in from the outside gets a definite vision of how these churches understand "family." They desire to inspire familial relationships that are based on loving one another and upholding their concepts of family values. This is often because they feel families and family values are under cultural assault, and as a result, they want it to be known that their church exists to empower families and familial bonds rather than indulging in worldly concepts of permissiveness and what they classify as questionable family values.

This all probably sounds great, right? Surely there is nothing wrong with teaching people about loving their families...is there? The problem is that these churches only teach on one kind of love, even if they seem to mention others. They might talk about loving one's neighbor or someone who is different from them, but if the only example or emphasis of visible love is on one's family, the people who are in that church are only going to learn how to love extensions of themselves: their families. There is certainly nothing wrong with it as a basic practice, but there is something wrong if all people are taught is about loving their immediate family and never coming to a place where we love others.

Familial love is an important aspect of learning foundational principles to being a successful person. When I say "successful," I don't mean becoming a millionaire, but becoming a productive, sincere, and yes, loving human being. Love doesn't mean much if there isn't any action associated with it, and if we make the mistake of assuming that we are enough "love" all by ourselves, we are going to find ourselves in some pretty difficult and disheartening relationships throughout our lives. Love is as much about giving as it is about receiving, and in families, we are given the opportunity to learn how all that works.

Here, in the comfort of those who are like we are in most ways, we can explore the ins and outs of the ways that relationships often impact personal identity and survival. We learn about sharing and caring, getting along with other people, the importance of teamwork, the sacrifices that love requires, what it takes to make life work, how we should treat other people, boundaries and space, and ultimately, the duty that we hold to those who are closest to us. In families, we ideally learn that we are special and that we can do more together if we have networks of support. God has given us family and familial alliance for this very reason. It's easier to learn about loving people who are very different from us if we first learn how to love people who are often very much like us. Having commonalities, such as the same ancestors, means we have some of the same likes, dislikes, and a common heritage that keeps things together. These commonalities give us a base by which to go by, and we can grow and develop our relationships from there.

BUT IF YOU REFUSE TO SERVE THE LORD, THEN CHOOSE TODAY WHOM YOU WILL SERVE. WOULD YOU PREFER THE GODS YOUR ANCESTORS SERVED BEYOND THE EUPHRATES? OR WILL IT BE THE GODS OF THE AMORITES IN WHOSE LAND YOU NOW LIVE? BUT AS FOR ME AND MY FAMILY, WE WILL SERVE THE LORD. (Joshua 24:15)

FOR THE SAKE OF MY FAMILY AND FRIENDS, I WILL SAY,
  "MAY YOU HAVE PEACE."
FOR THE SAKE OF THE HOUSE OF THE LORD OUR GOD,
  I WILL SEEK WHAT IS BEST FOR YOU, O JERUSALEM. (Psalm 122:8-9)

Family is not the only existence of love in this

world, however. It's awesome and great as a foundational place, as it creates a safe haven for learning and exploring the world of interpersonal relationships. This doesn't mean it's the only place of love in the world, and it means that when it comes to learning about love, we must balance familial love with other forms. We can easily get the idea from all these "family" churches that those we love – and those who love us – must always look like, sound like, and be exactly like we are. This is counter to love's call, and to learning to see the church as a family of Christ.

It's also important to recognize that not everyone has an ideal family unit or base of support from which to launch in their lives. Over-talking about family (taking it out of context or making it the only central point of a ministry, message, or work) can make those who haven't had this experience in their lives feel unwelcome or permanently damaged, as if they are beyond redemption or somehow so problematic, there is no hope for them. We must always remember to make room (in love, of course) for those who have had different situations and who have learned these skills in different ways, with different connections in their lives. There may be things they aren't sure about or are hesitant to dive into because they didn't have what someone else did, and instead of instituting a sort of bias against those who are without families, we need to remember our command to lift up children or family members who are alienated from others in their families or those who have been disowned, foster parents, adoptive parents, family members who step up to care for children who are not theirs, stepparents, friends who step up to take care of children, single parents, families who have a member with a disability, children who spend their lives caring for disabled or aging parents, and friends that become family, reminding us that there are all kinds of families, all kinds of people who are important in someone's life, and all sorts of people who contribute in different ways to help individuals become a functioning, part of society. Familial love shows up in many ways – and we should always be ready and willing to embrace such when it walks through our church doors.

Love isn't always unconditional (this side of heaven)

When we were little, someone probably told us about how we are loved for who we are (and not what we can do), and that they would love us unconditionally, no matter where we went or what we did. As we got older, we heard less about our family's unconditional love for us and more about what was expected of us in our family's rank, file, and situation. Under the guise of pleasing our parents, authority figures, or just doing our part in the family, we were expected to do our chores, get good grades in school, pay attention at church, play nice with our siblings, and do whatever we were taught was right. When we didn't measure up, we dealt with the reality that there were consequences for our behavior. I am not talking about our parents loving us enough to punish us (which is an important and responsible aspect of love); I am talking more about the realities of social pressure, even in families. When we don't do what we are supposed to be doing we deal with the fact that others don't always want to be around us. The more we act against our established familial norms, the more we will find ourselves isolated or separated from others. Suddenly, that unconditional promise we got as kids doesn't feel so "unconditional" anymore.

We might have also dealt with the conflict of watching our family tell us one thing but do something very different. Maybe we saw a sibling favored over us (or we were the favored sibling). Maybe our parents divorced or stayed together through intense marital discord. Maybe we had issues with someone in our family. Maybe we saw or experienced abuse or contention. No matter what happened, we saw facets and realities to familial situations that didn't feel, nor resemble, love. This might have confused or warped our concepts about love and made us believe that families and things related to familial love were false or somehow imaginary.

I think we often adopt fairy-tale concepts of love because fairy tales and fantasy love are our first in-book, in movie, on paper "definition" of what love is. It doesn't help that our families of origin are often complicated and confusing. Fairy-tale love is simpler and easier to accept and gives us a distorted view of reality when it comes to love. It's easy to look around and think that we aren't loved because we don't have a life that contrasts reality like Cinderella or Snow White. In those stories, familial love is often distorted and dysfunctional and is contrasted with the perfect love of a perfect person, who expects nothing of their mates or those around them. We reject the idea of expectation in love, assuming that in unconditional love, there is no forethought, and no expectation.

The problem with this is that fairy-tale love isn't reality. It doesn't prepare us for real life, and this contrasts with familial love, which is supposed to prepare us for real life. Even in the most ideal of family situations, something goes wrong somewhere, and someone instead of dealing with the facts that love (and our experience with love) is not as simple as we often hope it will be. It is in these places that we find the realities of expectation in love: to be loved we must also give love, and that is what separates the human experience of love from God's divine love toward us (although it does teach us about the importance of expressing and showing our love to others as recipients of divine love). Our families are teaching us that fairy-tale love doesn't exist, and if we are to have successful relationships with other people, sometimes we have to do things, endure things, and address things that might not always be pleasant-feeling or fun because that is what love does.

CHILDREN, OBEY YOUR PARENTS BECAUSE YOU BELONG TO THE LORD, FOR THIS IS THE RIGHT THING TO DO. "HONOR YOUR FATHER AND MOTHER." THIS IS THE FIRST COMMANDMENT WITH A PROMISE: IF YOU HONOR YOUR FATHER AND MOTHER, "THINGS WILL GO WELL FOR YOU, AND YOU WILL HAVE A LONG LIFE ON THE EARTH."

Dr. Lee Ann B. Marino, Ph.D., D.Min., D.D.

FATHERS, DO NOT PROVOKE YOUR CHILDREN TO ANGER BY THE WAY YOU TREAT THEM. RATHER, BRING THEM UP WITH THE DISCIPLINE AND INSTRUCTION THAT COMES FROM THE LORD. (Ephesians 6:1-4)

Thus, familial love is deeply rooted in a sense of obligation and responsibility. It teaches us about the duty of love: love isn't something we run wild with as a feeling or emotion, but a commitment that we make to see things through and behave in a manner that respects others and does our share. If we are to be a part of a bigger, loving community, we can't abandon ourselves to the hopes and dreams of fantasy people. People are imperfect and difficult and often do not love without condition. If we seek to be loved within this world, we must make ourselves lovable to those closest to us. This forces us to share, to help out as needed, to care for others, to keep our word, and to fulfill our responsibilities to others as a member of a larger unit.

Duty and responsibility to family

In modern culture, it's not uncommon to see families scattered all over a country (or perhaps, even the world). This was not the case in older times. When families relocated, they often relocated as a group (when such was possible) and people seldom left the city or region of their birth in their lifetimes. Life was slower, less complicated, and more focused on the people who might be in front of you versus those you didn't know who were far away.

Created For Love

Biblical families were much larger than our nuclear families today. Families weren't just parents and immediate children, but were parents, grandparents, aunts, uncles, cousins, siblings, and other distant relatives, all who held a certain position and status within the family. Status within the family usually descended, with older and first-born male members carrying most of the rights and responsibilities, followed by others. Older members were seen as having the duty to teach younger members the "right way," and if a younger member of the family went wayward, it was usually seen as a failure or irresponsibility on the part of an older member. Women were seen as responsible for care of homes, families, and as bearers of children, thus continuing the line. It was uncommon to see women step up in a leadership role among male relatives.

Ancient people were very literal in their understanding of familial duty and responsibility. These different codes and guidelines kept families bound together, establishing rules within their own to guide one another between differing generations. This means families were very dependent on one another to continue their livelihoods and survival from year to year. Many ancient societies developed specific codes of life and conduct that revolved around duties to families and familial honor in the hope that such would build strong communities and leave no member of a community without connection, means, or support. Many of these codes were rather rigid, assigning care, tasks, and financial support to various familial members, as well as assigning duties as pertaining to marital arrangements, family communication and contact, and the rights, rules, and regulations of families among themselves.

In some parts of the world, family codes like those of old still exist. It's not uncommon to hear about familial elders or "heads" making specific decisions as pertain to the entire group or clan, and you may occasionally meet someone in travel or internet social networking who speaks of arranged marriage or placing a heavy emphasis on their relationship with their parents in connection to their personal choices. This may seem hard to fathom in our modern mindsets, but they echo more of the method and interaction of families in Biblical times, out of which many of the writings and traditions of family are found.

While we live in different times and different circumstances today, this isn't to say that where we are at in our familial connections is wrong, or that we should go back to tribes and clan heads as we are overseen by a group of older family members we don't know very well. It also doesn't mean that we should go back in time to never leaving our cities or never making decisions for ourselves as adults without parental consent or input. What it does mean is that if we love our families, we should make a point to see familial interest as a part of our duty and responsibility.

I'm the first to admit that family doesn't always go the way we want, and that sometimes it is necessary to disconnect from family members who might be toxic or otherwise in a place where contact is not healthy, nor feasible. There is nothing wrong with doing this when it becomes necessary, because such will threaten our relationship with God and with others in our lives who are not toxic. But there are many instances where we just don't make the effort to connect with our families or care for them because we see ourselves as too busy or not having the time. We miss important events, we fail to make phone calls or send messages, we forget about birthdays and other special days, and the more and more that we distance ourselves from our families, the more we forget that if we love them, we have an obligation to do things that show such love.

BUT THOSE WHO WON'T CARE FOR THEIR RELATIVES, ESPECIALLY THOSE IN THEIR OWN HOUSEHOLD, HAVE DENIED THE TRUE FAITH. SUCH PEOPLE ARE WORSE THAN UNBELIEVERS. (1 Timothy 5:8)

The Scriptures are clear that if we won't care for what is closest to us, it makes us worse in the eyes of God than someone who isn't a believer in the faith. This is because our foundations of love – and love as an action, rather than a nice musing – are found right here, in how we care for those who we claim to love most. We can't ever make the excuse that we are just too busy, too swamped, or too uninterested to extend true love and care for those who are closest to us. What does care and love mean in this instance?

- Parents and guardians should be responsible for the needs of minor children in their care. These needs include food and shelter, physical, emotional and spiritual development, and financial responsibility, among others that may fall under these general categories.

- Adult children and other younger adult family members should be responsible to care for elderly or aging parents and other relatives as they find themselves unable to take care of themselves. This doesn't mean children should treat their parents or older relatives as if they are children, nor does it mean that the responsibility of caring for older relatives should fall on only one individual. It also doesn't mean that it is wrong to place older relatives in assisted living or other care if their well-being, regular care, and safety is beyond what a family member can provide. What it does mean is that younger family members are connected enough to the older members of their families to know when difficult decisions must be made and to provide love and encouragement throughout such situations.

- Immediate families should always spend time together. It does not have to be so scheduled as many do today, but can include family mealtimes, prayer times, Bible studies, or other family group events.

- We should make a point to be in contact with our relatives, however is best and works for everyone involved. It should be our pleasure to share different life events and successes of our relatives. This should never be one-sided, and it shouldn't be a situation where one person is doing all the sharing and others never reach out. A balance should exist if love is present.

- Family doesn't just mean our immediate, nuclear family but anyone to whom we are connected by "blood," as people call it. We should be open to meeting and interacting with more distant relatives just as much as we are with our immediate family. Such connects us to our natural heritage and our ancestors and familial traditions, giving us a sense of identity and placement within this world (in a natural sense)

- It should never be our prerogative to judge someone else's family or family situation based on our own. Just because someone's situation doesn't mirror our concept of care for others doesn't mean they don't, and it is very possible they do not have a family or relatives to reach out to in love.

Consider family a "starting ground" for learning to interact with and love others. If we aren't willing to do for those we are close to, we will be unwilling to do for those we don't know and don't care about. That's what the Apostle Paul emphasized the importance of caring for families as part of the life of believers. We should never get so quick in ourselves and our own personal ideal systems to think that we can abandon others in the hopes that God will understand our reasons. Such is contrary to the love we are called to walk in as Christians.

Respecting life

One of the most well-known commandments in the Bible involves parents. It's taught to children from a young age and recited to older individuals when they encounter issues with their families. It's a source of question and debate when parents abandon their children and in case of adoption. What is it – and what does it teach us about life and love?

HONOR YOUR FATHER AND MOTHER. THEN YOU WILL LIVE A LONG, FULL LIFE IN THE LAND THE LORD YOUR GOD IS GIVING YOU. (Exodus 20:12)

HONOR YOUR FATHER AND MOTHER, AS THE LORD YOUR GOD COMMANDED YOU. THEN YOU WILL LIVE A LONG, FULL LIFE IN THE LAND THE LORD YOUR GOD IS GIVING YOU. (Deuteronomy 5:16)

The command to honor one's father and mother is a foundational point in familial love and honor, not because we always agree with our parents, but because they were the ones who brought us into this natural world. In ancient times, honor of the ancestors was a common practice, often to the point of worshipping them. Ancestral worship existed (and still does, in some places) because ancestors were seen as a part of one's link to eternity. Honoring the past was a part of honoring the future, because had the ancestors never existed, neither would we, because we would have never been born. It was a part of the life cycle, recognizing the role that each and every one of us plays in eternity, and participating in the connectedness of life, rather than the disconnectedness we often feel.

We know that, as believers in the true God, worshipping our ancestors takes things too far and is not something we should do. The Scriptures, however, make complete provision for us to honor where we come from without going to the extreme of idolatry. We are given the expressed and specific command to honor our parents, with the promise if we do so, we too will live to be elders in the land and to receive our full inheritance this side of heaven.

What does this mean for us as believers and for those who don't have traditional families? That is a good question, because this passage has been used in all sorts of ways, including to bash or put down those who don't have the best relationship or any relationship with their biological parents. That is not God's purpose, nor His intent, in this passage. What God is showing us is familial love is about origins and about respecting the very foundations of life that are a part of every person's being. As human beings, we have ancestors. We are a part of the circle of life that shall continue long after we are gone. If we step up to respect the life that came before us, we are celebrating and standing in God's promise that is there for all of us. We recognize our ancestors didn't do everything right, and neither do we, but as we honor life, we honor what God did before we were ever here, is doing within us, what He will do through us, and what is to come after us.

This means that honoring our father and mother is honoring life: having a sense of honor and respect for order, for those who go before us, recognizing our life came through them and having the opportunity to be a part of this world, discovering the love of God and love of one another. In honoring such, we respect and are grateful that we are here. Honoring father and mother is about honoring all life that comes forth: natural and biological, spiritual, those who nurture and raise us (thus creating new points of origin for us if such is different from our biology), those who instruct and care about us, and who have positions of authority in our lives. When we appreciate foundations we appreciate God's creation, and we appreciate the work He does through people, even if they don't understand it themselves.

Thus, honoring our father and mother (our ancestors and elders) isn't about them. It's recognizing what God has done through them, and recognizing that God is our very foundation, no matter what happens with our biological families. Long before they ever thought about us, He did, and He knew that we would be placed here, on this earth, through their natural lineage. Whenever we step back to thank God that we are here, we honor our ancestors, as well as all who have helped to make us who we are, showing a true love for family in every literal sense of the word.

Different kinds of families

The extended family of ancient times makes us very aware that the exclusionary attitude we have about family today is very unbiblical. If you only define "family" as parents with a few children and a couple of pets, you are missing out on the entirety of family and the principle of family as was found in Biblical times. Even in the Bible, we see many kinds of families that inspire us to expand our view of "family" and the honor, responsibilities, and duties therein.

- **Abram** was close to his nephew, Lot (Genesis 12:5).

- **Tamar** was a single mother, giving birth to twins because of a one-time intimate encounter with her father-in-law to restore levirate inheritance in her family (Genesis 38:1-30).

- **Moses** was raised by Pharaoh's daughter, as an Egyptian rather than a Hebrew (Exodus 2:1-10).

- **Rizpah** interceded and buried the bodies of both her biological children (as a concubine) and the children of Merab, Saul's daughter (2 Samuel 21:8-13).

- **Esther** was raised by a relative, Mordecai (Esther 2:7).

- **Hosea** raised children that were possibly not even his (Hosea 1:2-9).

- **Jesus** was born to an unwed mother; many believe Joseph died when Jesus was young (Matthew 1:19-25).

- **Lydia** was head of a female-led household (Acts 16:11-15).

We never think about these different Biblical families as being a part of our lives today, because we treat them as if they are exceptions to the rule. The reality is that much of the Bible's prized families, held up as examples of morality, were just as dysfunctional as we are now. They were human beings, just as we are, and they were screwed up, led astray by cultural decisions, made bad choices, and didn't do things right. These examples are there to ease our confusions about those who don't come from "standard" family situations. They are there to ease our self-criticism and personal judgments of others, to make us realize that before God we are all equal, and we all have the same right and opportunity to serve Him if that is what we desire to do. No one should ever feel ashamed before God because of the situations they encountered thanks to their families of origin. It's all right to come from a different family; it's all right to have a different family; it's all right to be different.

LIVE A LIFE FILLED WITH LOVE, FOLLOWING THE EXAMPLE OF CHRIST. HE LOVED US AND OFFERED HIMSELF AS A SACRIFICE FOR US, A PLEASING AROMA TO GOD. (Ephesians 5:2)

PEACE BE WITH YOU, DEAR BROTHERS AND SISTERS, AND MAY GOD THE FATHER AND THE LORD JESUS CHRIST GIVE YOU LOVE WITH FAITHFULNESS. (Ephesians 6:23)

We are called to love those from different families just as we would anyone else who comes to us in faith. Church, Christianity, God, Christ, the faith aren't for those who are "perfect" in every possible way. We are here for the healing of those who hurt, the dead who need to come back to life, and the broken who need restoration. If we only attract those who we feel make the best impression or look the best on paper, we are ignoring an essential part of the Gospel's proclamation.

Disagreements

Yes, families are a launching ground for learning to get along and handle expressions of love. We learn there are different kinds of love by watching our families and other families, and we learn how to express different forms of love and honor among our relatives. Still, there is one area of love that we are supposed to learn as a starting place among our families...that we trip up, often, most of the time. That area is disagreement.

When I first considered being in ministry about twenty years back, I felt unqualified because my family of origin was a mess. No one was talking to each other and we just felt...so...obviously dysfunctional. I was used to getting postcards in the mail from pastors who looked picture perfect with their families in tow, sometimes even with their extended families or adult siblings. It all looked so picture perfect as everyone dressed the part and no one's hair was out of place. Then we had me, whose hair was always out of place and only one family member to stand in the picture with me. I felt like I was doing something wrong because I just didn't have and didn't look like everyone else.

Now with social media, I imagine there are an awful lot of people who feel the same way. I sit sometimes and look at people's family pictures and deal with the reality that many of them are probably not what they look like in visual print. It takes nothing to smile for the camera for a few minutes, only to resume a life of disagreement and unhappiness because we are glorifying a concept of "family" that was never what God intended. Just because you see a picture doesn't mean any love is really there and recognizing this was something that changed my life. I don't have to look like a fantasy picture to be real or relevant for God, and it bespeaks much more to those who embrace and love this ministry that I can say I have a family that's not a portrait, because by doing so I affirm that my life is real and I understand what it's like to live with disagreement rather than misguided, nonexistent perfection.

Human beings are human beings, and just because we are from the same family and we have some sort of similar genetic make-up doesn't mean we have everything in common, agree about things, or get along all the time. In fact, the Bible is quite expressive about familial disagreements. The more people you bring into a family, the more disagreements that exist. Ideally, we should learn how to speak to one another and how to sort through problems. Yet even the Bible admits this doesn't always happen, and sometimes division is the very real result.

A BROTHER WILL BETRAY HIS BROTHER TO DEATH, A FATHER WILL BETRAY HIS OWN CHILD, AND CHILDREN WILL REBEL AGAINST THEIR PARENTS AND CAUSE THEM TO BE KILLED...DON'T IMAGINE THAT I CAME TO BRING PEACE TO THE EARTH! I CAME NOT TO BRING PEACE, BUT A SWORD.

'I HAVE COME TO SET A MAN AGAINST HIS FATHER,
A DAUGHTER AGAINST HER MOTHER,
AND A DAUGHTER-IN-LAW AGAINST HER MOTHER-IN-LAW.

YOUR ENEMIES WILL BE RIGHT IN YOUR OWN HOUSEHOLD!'
"IF YOU LOVE YOUR FATHER OR MOTHER MORE THAN YOU LOVE ME, YOU ARE NOT WORTHY OF BEING MINE; OR IF YOU LOVE YOUR SON OR DAUGHTER MORE THAN ME, YOU ARE NOT WORTHY OF BEING MINE. IF YOU REFUSE TO TAKE

UP YOUR CROSS AND FOLLOW ME, YOU ARE NOT WORTHY OF BEING MINE. IF YOU CLING TO YOUR LIFE, YOU WILL LOSE IT; BUT IF YOU GIVE UP YOUR LIFE FOR ME, YOU WILL FIND IT.
(Matthew 10:21, 34-38)

There are two things Jesus acknowledges in this passage. The first is that families do not always get along, and division can be part of family life. The second is that in this life we are sometimes forced to make choices that seem to violate everything God put into place through natural relationships and principles. The results don't go with what we think should happen or should exist. It's our mistake to assume that just because a family exists, it should be unified and harmonized, because we don't see much of that in the families in Scripture. We see conflicts and difficulties, being forced to overcome problems and differences, and sometimes it seems like it worked out, but often the issues of the forefront passed away to become something else, something different.

We assume conflict is not a part of familial life because we misjudge its love for other forms of love that stress overcoming such behaviors. Familial love is not about us as individuals, but about us as a part of a unit (which we will speak of next). It teaches us how to be a part of a group, and ideally, how to work together. In the end, this usually means fighting for a common goal, even if we don't agree with others. But the other side to this is that familial love often loves itself, or its own image. Our families often have an image of us as an extension of them, not as people in our own right. The result is opposition and disagreement that isn't always as easily worked out as striving to stay together because you are a family. If we don't grow to embrace different forms of love, even among our families as we mature, we will find ourselves in a family situation that enmeshes our identities and leads to internal rebellion and dissolution.

HATRED STIRS UP QUARRELS, BUT LOVE MAKES UP FOR ALL OFFENSES. (Proverbs 10:12)

Familial love is a great starting point, but it is not enough to make a family successful as individual people. If we are going to be people that grow to embrace others as people (including our family members), we must grow to respect different boundaries and differences we have. Sometimes it means re-learning an entire relationship we thought we had with someone throughout our entire lives, coming to respect and admire them as a person. It might seem difficult and awkward at first, but to continue with familial growth and unity, we must bring different kinds of love into our family units.

When our families don't receive us

It's fine to recognize familial love as an important part of our lives on earth and in our introductions to love. Families and family relationships teach us many things that help us throughout our lives. Even if we are in a situation where our family life wasn't ideal, we can still learn many things about what not to do and what to do from interacting and watching others. Still, there is an answer to our familial origins that we often try to overlook or ignore, and that is the situation when our families don't accept who we are or accept something about us. They might claim to love us but pick us apart; they might say they are all right with us, but take every opportunity to criticize things about us that they find disapproving; or they might not even try to make pleasantries or express any sort of affection, but do nothing more than criticize and condemn. It might be a way that the relationship is standardized, a general feeling of disapproval and dislike, for any number of reasons that are far too numerous to list here.

Familial love doesn't always move beyond the familial alliance point. When we recognize familial love is something that keeps people together as a unit for base survival, the individual isn't always regarded as much on their own. Developing love for an individual person is a different process, and families don't always "get it" like we might hope. Sometimes our families love their concept of themselves in us, of their existing image in us, and never recognize us as individuals well enough to see us as separate from them, with our own uniqueness and individuality. This can cause a tightened grip, as they forever worry about something we do is going to make someone else see them badly.

As we grow as people, we develop a deep need to stand on our own and be recognized as whoever we have become (and who we desire to become). We want to be seen as individuals, as people with our own thoughts and ideas, and hope that as we come into our own, our family will continue to recognize and accept us as part of the bigger picture. Unfortunately, this doesn't always happen, and there is the expectation or social pressure within the family that you will change your mind or what you do if others in the family make life miserable enough for you.

If this isn't your experience, then be very thankful. If it is your experience, it can be difficult to bear and can lead to isolation from one's family. Our struggle for identity should never alienate us from our families, but it is something that does sometimes happen.

JESUS LEFT THAT PART OF THE COUNTRY AND RETURNED WITH HIS DISCIPLES TO NAZARETH, HIS HOMETOWN. THE NEXT SABBATH HE BEGAN TEACHING IN THE SYNAGOGUE, AND MANY WHO HEARD HIM WERE AMAZED. THEY ASKED, "WHERE DID HE GET ALL THIS WISDOM AND THE POWER TO PERFORM SUCH MIRACLES?" THEN THEY SCOFFED, "HE'S JUST A CARPENTER, THE SON OF MARY AND THE BROTHER OF JAMES, JOSEPH, JUDAS, AND SIMON. AND HIS SISTERS LIVE RIGHT HERE AMONG US." THEY WERE DEEPLY OFFENDED AND REFUSED TO BELIEVE IN HIM.

THEN JESUS TOLD THEM, "A PROPHET IS HONORED EVERYWHERE EXCEPT IN HIS OWN HOMETOWN AND AMONG HIS RELATIVES AND HIS OWN FAMILY." AND BECAUSE OF THEIR UNBELIEF, HE COULDN'T DO ANY MIRACLES AMONG THEM EXCEPT TO PLACE HIS HANDS ON A FEW SICK PEOPLE AND HEAL THEM.

AND HE WAS AMAZED AT THEIR UNBELIEF. (Mark 6:1-6)

Even Jesus Himself went through the experience of being both misunderstood and not fully accepted by His family. We don't quite know what specifics He is referring to within His natural family dynamic, but we can imagine that Jesus being Jesus, His ways and perceptions were not customary or en vogue with the times. This could lead to a great amount of disagreement and tension, as it would probably be unreasonable to suggest Jesus went through His early years without sharing any of His perspectives or teaching. We all know that little things and little ways of expressing, or ideals have a way of coming out, often in casual ways, and I am sure that when this happened, it often led to some conflict and disagreement with His immediate, devoutly Jewish family.

Our families of origin represent a starting point and a starting place for love and interaction with others, but it doesn't mean that where we start out is where we will wind up. Changes in our outlook, beliefs, feelings, opinions, and thoughts can take us far away from the places of origin that we thought would be there for us, no matter what happens. People are people, and disagreements sometimes cause divisions and separation.

If you are in a situation where your family has, in some way, disowned or disavowed you, know it happened to Jesus Himself, and our High Priest Who understands will connect you with others who can provide that familial feeling without being family biologically. We often say, "blood is thicker than water," but Spirit is stronger than blood. What we don't find from our families (or at least, find any longer) we can find in connection with other loving and supportive people who recognize where we are at and love us for who we are.

GOD PLACES THE LONELY IN FAMILIES;
HE SETS THE PRISONERS FREE AND GIVES THEM JOY.
BUT HE MAKES THE REBELLIOUS LIVE IN A SUN-SCORCHED LAND. (Psalm 68:6)

Friendship in a familial sense

We won't be looking at friendship very much in this chapter because love in friendship has an entire chapter, all its own, later in this book. We will, however, look briefly at connections that often feel much like family, even if we are not related to them by blood.

Not everyone we meet in our lives is family, but there are many who might love us like family, celebrating a long-term familial bond and relationship that is much like that of family. In ancient times, such bonds often became familial relations in a legal sense. Through the traditional forms of marital connection and dating, many familial and clan alliances turned into family through marital arrangements and familial agreements. This is why familial love might have been seen in a sense of a close, committed friendship, one that was deeper and more involved than that of an average acquaintance of casual bond. Loving some people like family was reserved for those who reflected the same issues, values, and priorities as a group, and for the importance of preserving that which is most important and most relevant for families.

There are two notable examples of familial friendship in the Bible: David and Jonathan and Ruth and Naomi. Both are important for their own reasons and display a love and commitment to one another in the face of adversity.

David and Jonathan were two individuals who, for all purposes, were destined to be enemies. According to birthright, Jonathan would be next in line as king, thus making him and David rivals for leadership of Israel. Jonathan was Saul's son, and by this time, David and Saul were enemies, and Saul even sought out David's life. Yet somehow, some way, Jonathan held allegiance to David over his own father, and the two forged a bond that sustained them through their lives and Jonathan's family line, even after Jonathan's death.

AFTER DAVID HAD FINISHED TALKING WITH SAUL, HE MET JONATHAN, THE KING'S SON. THERE WAS AN IMMEDIATE BOND BETWEEN THEM, FOR JONATHAN LOVED DAVID. FROM THAT DAY ON SAUL KEPT DAVID WITH HIM AND WOULDN'T LET HIM RETURN HOME. AND JONATHAN MADE A SOLEMN PACT WITH DAVID, BECAUSE HE LOVED HIM AS HE LOVED HIMSELF. JONATHAN SEALED THE PACT BY TAKING OFF HIS ROBE AND GIVING IT TO DAVID, TOGETHER WITH HIS TUNIC, SWORD, BOW, AND BELT. (1 Samuel

18:1-4)

Saul now urged his servants and his son Jonathan to assassinate David. But Jonathan, because of his strong affection for David, told him what his father was planning. "Tomorrow morning," he warned him, "you must find a hiding place out in the fields. I'll ask my father to go out there with me, and I'll talk to him about you. Then I'll tell you everything I can find out."

The next morning Jonathan spoke with his father about David, saying many good things about him. "The king must not sin against his servant David," Jonathan said. "He's never done anything to harm you. He has always helped you in any way he could. Have you forgotten about the time he risked his life to kill the Philistine giant and how the Lord brought a great victory to all Israel as a result? You were certainly happy about it then. Why should you murder an innocent man like David? There is no reason for it at all!"

So Saul listened to Jonathan and vowed, "As surely as the Lord lives, David will not be killed."

Afterward Jonathan called David and told him what had happened. Then he brought David to Saul, and David served in the court as before.

War broke out again after that, and David led his troops against the Philistines. He attacked them with such fury that they all ran away.

But one day when Saul was sitting at home, with spear in hand, the tormenting spirit from the Lord suddenly came upon him again. As David played his harp, Saul hurled his spear at David. But David dodged out of the way, and leaving the spear stuck in the wall, he fled and escaped into the night. (1 Samuel 19:1-10)

Then David took an oath before Jonathan and said, "Your father knows perfectly well about our friendship, so he has said to himself, 'I won't tell Jonathan—why should I hurt him?' But I swear to you that I am only a step away from death! I swear it by the Lord and by your own soul!"

"Tell me what I can do to help you," Jonathan exclaimed.

David replied, "Tomorrow we celebrate the New Moon festival. I've always eaten with the king on this occasion, but tomorrow I'll hide in the field and stay there until the evening of the third day. If your father asks where I am, tell him I asked permission to go home to Bethlehem for an annual family sacrifice. ⁷ If he says, 'Fine!' you will know all is well. But if he is angry and loses his temper, you will know he is determined to kill me. Show me this loyalty as my sworn friend—for we made a solemn pact before the Lord—or kill me yourself if I have sinned against your father. But please don't betray me to him!"

"Never!" Jonathan exclaimed. "You know that if I had the slightest notion my father was planning to kill you, I would tell you at once."

Then David asked, "How will I know whether or not your father is angry?"

"Come out to the field with me," Jonathan replied. And they went out there together. Then Jonathan told David, "I promise by the Lord, the God of Israel, that by this time tomorrow, or the next day at the latest, I will talk to my father and let you know at once how he feels about you. If he speaks favorably about you, I will let you know. But if he is angry and wants you killed, may the Lord strike me and even kill me if I don't warn you so you can escape and live. May the Lord be with you as he used to be with my father. And may you treat me with the faithful love of the Lord as long as I live. But if I die, treat my family with this faithful love, even when the Lord destroys all your enemies from the face of the earth."

So Jonathan made a solemn pact with David, saying, "May the Lord destroy all your enemies!" And Jonathan made David reaffirm his vow of friendship again, for Jonathan loved David as he loved himself. (1 Samuel 20:3-15)

One of the notable things about David and Jonathan is that there isn't much of an explanation for their connection. There was just something that seemed to draw them together and the power of their friendship overrode Jonathan's existing familial commitment to his father. His loyalties and interests were with David, and this is, most likely, in part because Jonathan knew the hand of God was upon David and the future of Israel rested with his leadership versus his father's. David and Jonathan became family and David continued to honor Jonathan's family even after his death, as is evident in seating Jonathan's son Mephibosheth at his royal table.

David and Jonathan created a bond of obligation, one that was sealed by covenant and maintained throughout life. They had similar values and ideals and were committed to the future of Israel as a nation. This gave them the necessary backing to operate as a family, even if it would seem like such a relationship was not meant to be.

Ruth and Naomi's story is a little different because they were family at one time but were not regarded as legally obligated family members when the story of Ruth opens in the Bible. Ruth and Naomi were mother-in-law and daughter-in-law by marriage, and all the men in their family – Naomi's husband, Ruth's husband, and Ruth's brother-in-law – had all died. This left behind three widowed women: Naomi, Ruth, and Orpah, Naomi's other daughter-in-law and Ruth's sister-in-law. Naomi was Jewish and living in Moab and Ruth was a Moabitess, a pagan woman from the nation where they were all living. Orpah went back to her family of origin, to find a new husband and a new life. Ruth, however, refused, pledging to remain with Naomi, instead.

But Ruth replied, "Don't ask me to leave you and turn back. Wherever you go, I will go; wherever you live, I will live. Your people will be my people, and your God will be my God. Wherever you die, I will die, and there I will be buried. May the Lord punish me severely if I allow anything but death to separate us!" When Naomi saw that Ruth was determined to go with her, she said nothing more. (Ruth 1:16-18)

I'm sure you are thinking, "but Ruth and Naomi were family!" This is true, and in ancient terms, it's not true. Even though Naomi and Ruth were related by marriage, they were no longer connected in their times because the marriage no longer existed. Because women were viewed as property, it was understood that they would return to their families of origin so a new marital arrangement could be made. Death broke the familial bonds, and that meant Ruth had no legal, nor societal, nor social responsibility or obligation to Naomi. Naomi would be a widow (as she was too old to bear children), bound to a family that no longer had much use for her, and not really having a place anymore in society, except as an outcast. Ruth's position, however, would be to return to her family of origin, and committing herself to remain with Naomi was neither customary, nor common.

What it was, however, was quite radical.

Ruth made a commitment to remain with and care for Naomi as if she was a part of her biological family, even though she was not. She extended familial love in friendship, one that went far beyond the normal interactions we have with our friends, even if we love them deeply. She returned to Bethlehem with her, labored for her well-being, and took care of both of them, even though doing such wasn't probably a lot of fun with an older, embittered woman.

One day Ruth the Moabite said to Naomi, "Let me go out into the harvest fields to pick up the stalks of grain left behind by anyone who is kind enough to let me do it."

Naomi replied, "All right, my daughter, go ahead." So Ruth went out to gather grain behind the harvesters. And as it happened, she found herself working in a field that belonged to Boaz, the relative of her father-in-law, Elimelech. (Ruth 2:2-3)

When Ruth went back to work again, Boaz ordered his young men, "Let her gather grain right among the sheaves without stopping her. And pull out some heads of barley from the bundles and drop them on purpose for her. Let her pick them up, and don't give her a hard time!"

So Ruth gathered barley there all day, and when she beat out the grain that evening, it filled an entire basket. She carried it back into town and showed it to her mother-in-law. Ruth also gave her the roasted grain that was left over from her meal.

"Where did you gather all this grain today?" Naomi asked. "Where did you work? May the Lord bless the one who helped you!"

So Ruth told her mother-in-law about the man in whose field she had worked. She said, "The man I worked with today is named Boaz."

"May the Lord bless him!" Naomi told her daughter-in-law. "He is showing his kindness to us as well as to your dead husband. That man is one of our closest relatives, one of our family redeemers."

Then Ruth said, "What's more, Boaz even told me to come back and stay with his harvesters until the entire harvest is completed."

"Good!" Naomi exclaimed. "Do as he said, my daughter. Stay with his young women right through the whole harvest. You might be harassed in other fields, but you'll be safe with him."

So Ruth worked alongside the women in Boaz's fields and gathered grain with them until the end of the barley harvest. Then she continued working with them through the wheat harvest in early summer. And

ALL THE WHILE SHE LIVED WITH HER MOTHER-IN-LAW. (Ruth 2:15-23)

In the end, Ruth and Naomi become literal family again through Ruth's marriage to Boaz, who was a kinsman-redeemer from Naomi's deceased husband's family.

THEN BOAZ SAID TO THE ELDERS AND TO THE CROWD STANDING AROUND, "YOU ARE WITNESSES THAT TODAY I HAVE BOUGHT FROM NAOMI ALL THE PROPERTY OF ELIMELECH, KILION, AND MAHLON. AND WITH THE LAND I HAVE ACQUIRED RUTH, THE MOABITE WIDOW OF MAHLON, TO BE MY WIFE. THIS WAY SHE CAN HAVE A SON TO CARRY ON THE FAMILY NAME OF HER DEAD HUSBAND AND TO INHERIT THE FAMILY PROPERTY HERE IN HIS HOMETOWN. YOU ARE ALL WITNESSES TODAY."

THEN THE ELDERS AND ALL THE PEOPLE STANDING IN THE GATE REPLIED, "WE ARE WITNESSES! MAY THE LORD MAKE THIS WOMAN WHO IS COMING INTO YOUR HOME LIKE RACHEL AND LEAH, FROM WHOM ALL THE NATION OF ISRAEL DESCENDED! MAY YOU PROSPER IN EPHRATHAH AND BE FAMOUS IN BETHLEHEM. AND MAY THE LORD GIVE YOU DESCENDANTS BY THIS YOUNG WOMAN WHO WILL BE LIKE THOSE OF OUR ANCESTOR PEREZ, THE SON OF TAMAR AND JUDAH."

SO BOAZ TOOK RUTH INTO HIS HOME, AND SHE BECAME HIS WIFE. WHEN HE SLEPT WITH HER, THE LORD ENABLED HER TO BECOME PREGNANT, AND SHE GAVE BIRTH TO A SON. THEN THE WOMEN OF THE TOWN SAID TO NAOMI, "PRAISE

THE LORD, WHO HAS NOW PROVIDED A REDEEMER FOR YOUR FAMILY! MAY THIS CHILD BE FAMOUS IN ISRAEL. MAY HE RESTORE YOUR YOUTH AND CARE FOR YOU IN YOUR OLD AGE. FOR HE IS THE SON OF YOUR DAUGHTER-IN-LAW WHO LOVES YOU AND HAS BEEN BETTER TO YOU THAN SEVEN SONS!"

NAOMI TOOK THE BABY AND CUDDLED HIM TO HER BREAST. AND SHE CARED FOR HIM AS IF HE WERE HER OWN. THE NEIGHBOR WOMEN SAID, "NOW AT LAST NAOMI HAS A SON AGAIN!" AND THEY NAMED HIM OBED. HE BECAME THE FATHER OF JESSE AND THE GRANDFATHER OF DAVID. (Ruth 4:9-17)

Even in Ruth's second marriage to Boaz, she never forgot Naomi. The two came together as family once again, bound for the purpose of life and friendship. Their connection took them far beyond where they started and shows us the power of commitment in friendships that lead us to a place of understanding true family and familial love. Family isn't always blood; sometimes it is the people who make us, who support us, and who care about us, against all odds.

Family of God

One of the reasons why familial love is so relevant is because we understand, as Christians, that we are a family: the family of God. This might sound odd, as it's not something we hear nearly enough about, but it is most definitely true. In fact, the only outright Biblical reference to a non-negative form of *storgay* (it is *phileostorgos*) in the New Testament is for the church, in Romans 12:10.

LOVE EACH OTHER WITH GENUINE AFFECTION, AND TAKE DELIGHT IN HONORING EACH OTHER.

The church is illustrated in this place because it is designed to be a starting launch for those of us who are believers on matters of spiritual life in this world. When we come into the church, we are spiritual babies who must learn how to do all things spiritual: we must learn how to walk as Christians, talk as Christians, interact with others as Christians, and start our lives again, all over. We figure these things out as we dwell with other believers who genuinely care about us, helping us to see things differently and grow as He destines us to do so.

The difference between our family of origins and our spiritual family is simple: our families of origin are designed to prefigure God's love, but they aren't the full interaction, nor example, of it in our lives. It comes with specific limitations and doesn't often live up to what it should. This can also happen in God's family, but it's not meant to be that way. As believers, we are to genuinely and sincerely care about others in the church as if they were our own blood relatives, as if they were reflections of everything we pride ourselves on as present in our family bonds. The difference is that these individuals aren't of our natural families, and that means in many ways, they are probably very different than we are. It is thanks to the work of God that we can stand and say we love our brothers and sisters in Christ, because God has come into our lives and transformed our priorities. Rather than struggling for survival and seeing everyone as an enemy, we can see family, we can see friends who have become our family, and we can realize that loving others doesn't have to be as difficult – or exclusive – as we sometimes find with others.

Yes, the potential is there, and we are commanded to walk in it, finding something special in our relationships with other believers that teaches us something about loving everyone else. It launches and encourages us and gives us the foundation to face the intimidating and difficult ins and outs of this world with true confidence. When we find our family in Christ, we find true family, and it reminds us that whether we are rejected by our family of origin, find ourselves in conflict with them, or just outgrow the limitations of that relationship, we can find genuine love and affection, a true place and sense of honor, and the realization of hope, because only God can take a group of strangers and turn them into His family, with the power to transform and change the entire world.

Reflections

- What grounding do we find in familial love and alliance?

- Why can family love be limiting?

- How does familial love extend beyond our own biological family?

- How does familial love relate to the body of believers?

- What can you learn from your own experience with familial love about love and about loving others in Christianity?

Chapter Three

DELIBERATE AFFECTION (*HESED*)

Hesed[1]

חֶסֶד checed {kheh'-sed}

Meanings:
- goodness
- kindness
- faithfulness
- a reproach, shame

WHEN words describing love are studied, seldom do we see the Hebrew word *hesed* make the cut. There are a few reasons for this: the primary one being it is often translated in alternate context, such as goodness, kindness, or faithfulness. Yet there is one term that *hesed* translates as that very much relates to love: lovingkindness or loving-kindness. This reveals a powerful heart and purpose behind *hesed*'s intent: it is more than just doing something to do it, but connecting back to the origin of love, its very foundation in why such things are done, and in how they can be done rightly and with good intent.

In this chapter, we are going to look at an overlooked aspect of love: that of *hesed*, of love that serves as the root for doing things that are good, faithful, and noble as we understand such in our faith. So many of us want to do good and noble things, but few of us are willing to take the time to learn the difference between doing things with love and just doing things to do them. What defines an action truly done in faith, versus one that is just done to prove something to others? The answer: *hesed*, actions done in a sense of love, rather than just doing things to try and show how wonderful someone is or how great they are. When we work in *hesed*, we are doing it for God, versus just doing it for us.

Properly defining hesed

Hesed is a Biblical term understood to have a depth to it that is not easily translated. Unlike some of the other terms we have looked at thus far, it's not because *hesed* is used to describe a blanket of things within its definition, thus making it a complicated word. *Hesed* is specific, referring to specific depths and ideals that reflect the best of the divine nature and encourage us to also partake of them ourselves. *Hesed* is more than just doing an action with no purpose or forethought to it. It describes careful and deliberate movements of faith, emphasizing loyalty and love within each action. It tells us much of God, Who is the source of *hesed*, and those who are His people who deliberately seek to walk in *hesed*. In the unique love of *hesed*, we never run out, fail, or give up, and such is evident in the powerful bonds that it creates.

For this reason, *hesed* is often translated by its attributes: goodness, faithfulness, and kindness. We also see it translated as "lovingkindness," which we will speak on a bit later. It is also sometimes used to describe a reproach or shame, identifying with *hesed* because kindness and goodness were required to counteract negative behavior. It helps us to realize that *hesed* is all of these things, rolled into one, and rolled into the actions that help others realize just how much God – and we – care about them.

Doing for others on purpose

If you hear a teaching on love today, the minister or speaker will, most likely, emphasize love as something that you do versus something that you feel. I think it is fair to say that the way we often see and hear about love in an entertainment context is often not described as something that's shown, but something, instead, that is felt, a concept or ideal that is within a person and that motivates a certain overflow of feeling as a result. It often looks like love is about having a certain feeling or impulse, something abstract and distant, rather than something applicable and concrete. This causes many to spend a lot of time looking for a feeling that will cause them to feel a specific way, rather than doing things that will help facilitate a certain sense of love and identity of such in one's life.

Well...it is true that love is something that we do and is almost always a verb in the Scriptures. *Hesed*, however, is a noun, not a verb. It is something that prompts something else, a state of being and identity, if you will, that motivates a certain expression. I suppose we can say that *hesed* is the prompt, the inclination, or yes, maybe even the feeling or sense that leads someone into a place of doing for others. In other words, *hesed* is something that someone can feel or experience, but it doesn't end there. In *hesed* we are motivated to do something with what we recognize to be present within, and we are moved to act upon it. It's not just a matter of feeling something, but the result of doing something because of a deeper prompting.

So, love is a little bit of both: it is something that we can feel or perceive, but it is something that also prompts a response. It doesn't just lay dormant within us and do nothing. True love doesn't just make us feel goofy or silly. True love prompts us to action; to do for others and to extend the true love we have received in kind. We know when it's there, and we know when it's not there. Its very presence helps us to realize there is a whole world out there that needs a touch other than the one it has, and seeks to extend a little bit of God's kindness toward everyone through the work of the Spirit within.

Love is something that extends to others in many different ways and forms. We tend to get hung up on two forms of love (romantic and familial) and ignore the many different ways love can manifest in a situation, often that don't fall into either of these categories. The majority of love that is shown in our lives is neither, because it manifests in the form of one person genuinely seeking to do good to another. It's something they do, on purpose, because they are prompted to do so through love.

ONE DAY DAVID ASKED, "IS ANYONE IN SAUL'S FAMILY STILL ALIVE—ANYONE TO WHOM I CAN SHOW KINDNESS FOR JONATHAN'S SAKE?" HE SUMMONED A MAN NAMED ZIBA, WHO HAD BEEN ONE OF SAUL'S SERVANTS. "ARE YOU ZIBA?" THE KING ASKED.

"YES SIR, I AM," ZIBA REPLIED.

THE KING THEN ASKED HIM, "IS ANYONE STILL ALIVE FROM SAUL'S FAMILY? IF SO, I WANT TO SHOW GOD'S KINDNESS TO THEM."

ZIBA REPLIED, "YES, ONE OF JONATHAN'S SONS IS STILL ALIVE. HE IS CRIPPLED IN BOTH FEET."
"WHERE IS HE?" THE KING ASKED.

"IN LO-DEBAR," ZIBA TOLD HIM, "AT THE HOME OF MAKIR SON OF AMMIEL."

SO DAVID SENT FOR HIM AND BROUGHT HIM FROM MAKIR'S HOME. HIS NAME WAS MEPHIBOSHETH; HE WAS JONATHAN'S SON AND SAUL'S GRANDSON. WHEN HE CAME TO DAVID, HE BOWED LOW TO THE GROUND IN DEEP RESPECT. DAVID SAID, "GREETINGS, MEPHIBOSHETH."

MEPHIBOSHETH REPLIED, "I AM YOUR SERVANT."

"Don't be afraid!" David said. "I intend to show kindness to you because of my promise to your father, Jonathan. I will give you all the property that once belonged to your grandfather Saul, and you will eat here with me at the king's table!"

Mephibosheth bowed respectfully and exclaimed, "Who is your servant, that you should show such kindness to a dead dog like me?"

Then the king summoned Saul's servant Ziba and said, "I have given your master's grandson everything that belonged to Saul and his family. You and your sons and servants are to farm the land for him to produce food for your master's household. But Mephibosheth, your master's grandson, will eat here at my table." (Ziba had fifteen sons and twenty servants.)

Ziba replied, "Yes, my lord the king; I am your servant, and I will do all that you have commanded." And from that time on, Mephibosheth ate regularly at David's table, like one of the king's own sons.

Mephibosheth had a young son named Mica. From then on, all the members of Ziba's household were Mephibosheth's servants. And Mephibosheth, who was crippled in both feet, lived in Jerusalem and ate regularly at the king's table. (2 Samuel 9:1-13)

We can recall the relationship between David

and Jonathan because we discussed it in the last chapter. The two of them forged a serious commitment, one that rendered them to have a familial bond even though they were not related. This meant that David and Jonathan expressed their love and care for one another by making the interests of the other a primary priority. They provided necessary information, took risks, and treated one another as if they were family. After Jonathan died, David continued this familial bond by reaching out to Mephibosheth, Jonathan's son. The Scriptures show us that David had to seek out Mephibosheth, because he was unable to walk and deformed in his feet. He was not easy to find, and David had to make the effort to show a sense of love – manifest in kindness – to him. David set out to keep his commitment and his word to Jonathan, and he did just that – seeking out and doing right by Mephibosheth, even though it wasn't easy and there are probably those who might have disapproved or wondered what he was doing.

The same is true for us when we seek to do the right thing in love and it is done without a romantic notion or emotional feeling. We do what is right because it is right, because God moves us to do it, and it manifests in the form of loving kindness, goodness, and faithfulness. God has given it to us, He has placed it within us, and now we, too, seek out that opportunity to pay it forward and do for others.

Why do you do what you do?

I grew up in a large, often legalistic

denomination that puts a heavy emphasis on works. We were encouraged from a very young age to be first in line to do things for others, especially the church. It was the responsibility of the laity to keep the church going financially and practically, and very little of the work within the church was done by paid clergy. The members of the church were required to clean it, prepare the different linens and garments used in services, handle readings and songs, and the other various lay ministries of the church, and handle the housekeeping and meal preparations for the ministers. Church members were also expected to volunteer in different social activities, such as homeless outreach or working in anti-abortion efforts. I grew up watching many women, very active and involved, in virtually everything they could get their hands on to do. They were doers; they believed in the power of doing, and somewhere because of their doctrine, they believed that doing good would help to save them. Doing things was a requirement of their faith.

This sounds good, right? It sounds idealistic and like much of what we are supposed to do, right? Well, there were a few realities behind this that made what they did go very seriously awry. It might sound idealistic on the surface, but because they were performing their actions to produce faith, there wasn't much behind why they did them. Their motivations weren't because God prompted something within them, but because they hoped such works would prompt something within their own seeking of faith and salvation. None of their works were an extension of their faith, but they were working their works to try and spark their faith.

The results were abysmal. It was hard to get volunteers for projects because the people who ran the show either didn't want anyone else to show them up or were so punitive, they made it impossible for others to participate in doing good. They were often grouchy and angry and did their works with a great deal of complaining and dissatisfaction. When things didn't go their way with a specific individual, they were quick to provide long detail of all the things they had done for someone. There was no joy in the things they did. They never found God in their actions, but hoped instead that God would result from them.

There are a lot of people who do things with this same motive and agenda in mind. They hope that the relationship with God they have always dreamed of or the faith they don't quite understand will come into focus if they do more things. While there is nothing wrong with being "a doer" and coming into a deeper relationship with God as you experience Him through action, there is something wrong with trying to constantly do things to find that relationship.

Love is central to our faith experience because the Scriptures teach us that God Himself is love. What God has done for us changes us because it is the very incarnation, the very reality of what love is, and what love does, in our lives. In our faith, we have received the love of God, and it has changed us. We might not be perfect, we might have times where we don't express it quite the way that we should, and there are probably moments where we all lapse in our judgments and falter before God. Despite this, the love of God draws us back and in, capturing our hearts and minds in a way that continually pours into us. This is the very foundation by which we walk with God and motivates us to do everything we do by faith.

Since God chose you to be the holy people he loves, you must clothe yourselves with tenderhearted mercy, kindness, humility, gentleness, and patience. Make allowance for each other's faults, and forgive anyone who offends you. Remember, the Lord forgave you, so you must forgive others. Above all, clothe yourselves with love, which binds us all together in perfect harmony. And let the peace that comes from Christ rule in your hearts. For as members of one body you are called to live in peace. And always be thankful.

Let the message about Christ, in all its richness, fill your lives. Teach and counsel each other with all the wisdom he gives. Sing psalms and hymns and spiritual songs to God with thankful hearts. And whatever you do or say, do it as a representative of the Lord Jesus, giving thanks through Him to God the Father. (Colossians 3:12-17)

As we learn more about love as a central part to our faith experience, we come to realize that if love has transformed us and we receive that understanding by faith, we want to do something with what we have received from God. Our works come from this foundation: it's not that we are saved by them or believe they can save us, but that we can't keep what God has done for us to ourselves. We want to give out some of what we have received. As God works in our lives and transforms us from glory to glory and faith to faith, we do what we do because we can't help ourselves: God's love makes us want to do more and more for others.

Hesed makes us consider our actions and our behaviors, thoughtfully and carefully. We can do the greatest deeds in the world and do them without the love of God behind them. The Scriptures, however, mandate our works to come from a base of love if they are to make a difference. We must do what we do out of love, or else our works don't count. Such love demands a careful inventory of our motives, assessing and considering the realities of why we do what we do. It is useful for us to sit back and consider our prompts and purposes in Christ, and as we look over the things we do, assess our relationship with God in the process. It's a marker; an examiner; and a truth-teller about our true priorities and prompts behind every one of our actions.

The problem with do-gooders

We've all met them: people who seem, at least on the surface, to be at the forefront of every cause. They are the cheerleaders for everything that seems to be right. They might espouse a ton of personal causes and are volunteers for all of them. They claim to be all right with everything, desire to help with everything, and believe in everything. Somehow, they manage to make everyone else look bad, not committed enough, or involved enough. They are do-gooders, individuals who take on the causes of the world, and are often the first in line to support many things.

Anyone who has met one knows do-gooders can be a bit much to take because it's hard to keep up with them. In fact, we might easily feel bad when we compare ourselves to them. I remember when I met a do-gooder early on in my ministry; wow, how awful I felt in comparison to her. She was doing everything, running here, running there, the forefront of every cause, the first at all the conferences, the most sought-after of all the speakers. I looked at my little ministry and my small itinerary and felt nearly invisible next to her.

Do-gooders tend to have that effect on us...have you ever wondered why? It's like whenever we stand next to one of them, we feel small and unimportant. Actually, that's exactly the purpose and point of someone who seeks to be a do-gooder in their lives. The difference between a do-gooder and someone who makes the effort to do good is the heart motivation behind it. Do-gooders seek to edify and draw attention to themselves.

WATCH OUT! DON'T DO YOUR GOOD DEEDS PUBLICLY, TO BE ADMIRED BY OTHERS, FOR YOU WILL LOSE THE REWARD FROM YOUR FATHER IN HEAVEN. WHEN YOU GIVE TO SOMEONE IN NEED,

DON'T DO AS THE HYPOCRITES DO—BLOWING TRUMPETS IN THE SYNAGOGUES AND STREETS TO CALL ATTENTION TO THEIR ACTS OF CHARITY! I TELL YOU THE TRUTH, THEY HAVE RECEIVED ALL THE REWARD THEY WILL EVER GET. BUT WHEN YOU GIVE TO SOMEONE IN NEED, DON'T LET YOUR LEFT HAND KNOW WHAT YOUR RIGHT HAND IS DOING. GIVE YOUR GIFTS IN PRIVATE, AND YOUR FATHER, WHO SEES EVERYTHING, WILL REWARD YOU. (Matthew 6:1-4)

We read the Scriptures and hear the behavior of the Pharisees and find it almost laughable. We can't believe anyone was so vain to give to the poor with a trumpet procession behind them, all to call attention to their good deeds. Yet isn't that just how a do-gooder tends to be about whatever good they are doing? Maybe they don't walk around with a full orchestra in their midst, but they like to pose nicely for the camera, or speak up for a cause so others notice, or to get the most attention for the things they do. They often don't work and play well with others, because no matter how much they scream their support, it's different when you must do things and no one is looking.

Let's understand that there is nothing wrong with accepting a compliment (such as someone who desires to laud you for something you've done), with advocating for a cause and becoming a visible voice for it, or for being photographed doing something for others. None of these things are wrong in and of themselves. It wasn't the reality of outside admiration that was wrong when it came to the Pharisees and their behaviors; it was the

Pharisees themselves, who were manipulating circumstances to get attention. The reason for this is that their heart isn't right, much like the Pharisees' hearts weren't right. They were doing good things to get noticed, to get the attention of others, and to have others think they were wonderful or superior in some way. It wasn't about the giving, but about what would come out of the praise and attention from others for the giving. Jesus used the Pharisees as an example of giving gone awry, of people who do very good things with very selfish motives. The hope – and expectation – is that those who hear Jesus' words (even unto the present day) will consider why they do what they do and realize that if we aren't doing good deeds for the right reason, it doesn't count (nor produce spiritual fruit) like we would like it to.

If we want things to make a difference in the lives of others, we must be sincere. To be sincere, we must come from a place of love. What we do, every action we take, must be motivated by a genuine sense of the wholesome goodness God has placed within each of us as believers. Our actions are to come from a deep desire to express a sense of love, of well-being and change, to a world that is often self-seeking and self-centered. When we have God, we understand every need we have shall be met by faith, thus enabling us to do for others without condition or cost, and with the true hope and promise that things can get better for all of us if we are willing to do all out of our sense of grounding and transforming love.

Works done right

Doing what we do from a place of love doesn't mean we have to do everything for others all by ourselves. It also doesn't mean that we should sit around and do nothing in the hopes that our "love" needs to kick in first. While we've spent time looking at the wrong motives that may come from in their service to others, I can't deny there are too many people who aren't doing enough. Our faith requires both maintenance and a sense of smart balance, and that means we shouldn't ever get comfortable in assuming that the words of the Scriptures are for "someone else." If you're the one reading it, inventory is always an important and we should always consider we can examine and receive the Word in a new and different way. This is especially true when it comes to all issues pertaining to the expression of our faith. It's tempting to read the Scriptures in one exclusive context or another, and those contexts tend to side in our favor. We don't like to entertain that maybe, just maybe, we need a good, solid jolt of love in our lives and that our actions should show it in a more radical way.

WHAT GOOD IS IT, DEAR BROTHERS AND SISTERS, IF YOU SAY YOU HAVE FAITH BUT DON'T SHOW IT BY YOUR ACTIONS? CAN THAT KIND OF FAITH SAVE ANYONE? SUPPOSE YOU SEE A BROTHER OR SISTER WHO HAS NO FOOD OR CLOTHING, AND YOU SAY, "GOOD-BYE AND HAVE A GOOD DAY; STAY WARM AND EAT WELL"—BUT THEN YOU DON'T GIVE THAT PERSON ANY FOOD OR CLOTHING. WHAT GOOD DOES THAT DO?

So you see, faith by itself isn't enough. Unless it produces good deeds, it is dead and useless.

Now someone may argue, "Some people have faith; others have good deeds." But I say, "How can you show me your faith if you don't have good deeds? I will show you my faith by my good deeds."

You say you have faith, for you believe that there is one God. Good for you! Even the demons believe this, and they tremble in terror. How foolish! Can't you see that faith without good deeds is useless?

Don't you remember that our ancestor Abraham was shown to be right with God by his actions when he offered his son Isaac on the altar? You see, his faith and his actions worked together. His actions made his faith complete. And so it happened just as the Scriptures say: "Abraham believed God, and God counted him as righteous because of his faith." He was even called the friend of God.

So you see, we are shown to be right with God by what we do, not by faith alone.

Rahab the prostitute is another example. She was shown to be right with God by her actions when she hid those messengers and sent them safely away by a different road. Just as the body is dead without breath, so also faith is dead without good works. (James 2:14-26)

The arguments over faith and works date back to those who believed they could work their way into heaven by good deeds. By doing such, they were rejecting the necessity of Christ in their salvation. Yet we can see something important if we take the Apostle James' words along with those of the Apostle Paul about faith: there have always been people on both sides of the debate in extreme ruts. Some are all about what they do, and some think they have to do nothing. The truth of the matter is the answer in the middle: yes, we are not saved by our works; yes, we are transformed by our faith; and yes, our faith prompts and inspires us to good works. All three are true, and none of those three contradict one another. We need all three to have a complete spiritual experience, one that enhances and grows our faith, and develops a sense of outlook and gratitude within us. Works done right comes through our faith, which stirs us to greater things and to greater insights. It's all a part of God's plan for us, and our cooperation with His work, deep within us.

Being drawn

I've often described the relationships that we have in the Spirit as a "drawing." God draws us to Him as we are led and moved to do so through Christ Jesus, and we are also drawn to one another as believers: we are drawn to our leaders, our leaders are drawn to us, and we are drawn to our brothers and sisters in Christ. It is an entire process that may seem mystical and deeply spiritual to us, but it has an important root that keeps it functioning. It is the very spiritual presence, the power of God that is at work in drawing us by what the Bible calls "loving kindness." A variation of this term is often how the word *hesed* is translated into English.

The term "lovingkindness" is found twenty-nine times in the King James Version of the Bible. It is not always translated as such in other translations, but has a certain melodic ring to it that inspires people from generation to generation with its ideals. There's just something about "lovingkindness," probably because it links together a purpose as well as an expression: it is love, and it is kind. The phrase perfectly emphasizes that it is love that seeks out the best for us, and expresses itself in a manner that we can all relate to, respond to, and accept in our lives.

SHEW THY MARVELLOUS LOVINGKINDNESS, O THOU THAT SAVEST BY THY RIGHT HAND THEM WHICH PUT THEIR TRUST IN THEE FROM THOSE THAT RISE UP AGAINST THEM. (Psalm 17:7, KJV)

HOW EXCELLENT IS THY LOVINGKINDNESS, O GOD! THEREFORE THE CHILDREN OF MEN PUT THEIR TRUST UNDER THE SHADOW OF THY WINGS. (Psalm 36:7, KJV)

YET THE LORD WILL COMMAND HIS LOVINGKINDNESS IN THE DAY TIME, AND IN THE NIGHT HIS SONG SHALL BE WITH ME, AND MY PRAYER UNTO THE GOD OF MY LIFE. (Psalm 42:8, KJV)

BECAUSE THY LOVINGKINDNESS IS BETTER THAN LIFE, MY LIPS SHALL PRAISE THEE. (Psalm 63:3, KJV)

THE LORD HATH APPEARED OF OLD UNTO ME, SAYING, YEA, I HAVE LOVED THEE WITH AN EVERLASTING LOVE: THEREFORE WITH LOVINGKINDNESS HAVE I DRAWN THEE. (Jeremiah 31:3, KJV)

AND I WILL BETROTH THEE UNTO ME FOR EVER; YEA, I WILL BETROTH THEE UNTO ME IN RIGHTEOUSNESS, AND IN JUDGMENT, AND IN LOVINGKINDNESS, AND IN MERCIES. (Hosea 2:19, KJV)

The loving kindness of God draws us to Him and then from Him we learn about loving kindness – our love put into action – from God Himself. God draws us to Him through loving kindness, through a love shown and put into practical action. God doesn't draw us as we hear about fire and brimstone or a severe fear of hell or going to hell, but by showing us His love for us. It is real and active, put into practice and manifest in the different ways that He is good and kind to us. The love of God fills us, gives us an experience that is genuine and honest, and in turn, we desire to turn around and pour the love of God into the lives of others, practically, not abstractly.

Still, this love starts with something that we've received from Him. It's something that we can feel and recognize, and we know when it is present in our lives by our awareness of it. Lovingkindness is a part of our relationship with God, a realization that in

God's great love to us, He expresses it. This is what separates the true God from false idols, and Christianity from false theologies or ideals. It's improbable to state that God loves His creation but is totally devoid and disinterested in what happens to those who are in it. God's love is active; it does toward us and for us, seeking to do good and enhance life.

It is God, therefore, Who teaches us in lovingkindness how to interact with others. Thinking that we will draw people by being nasty, punitive, and overly intense is a misnomer. I understand that we think "fire and brimstone" and "holiness or hell" has a certain spiritual effectiveness to it, but in reality, it doesn't. People who come around to the thinking out of fear don't stick with it and others wind up alienated and disgusted. It is far more effective to follow God's lead on loving kindness and draw people in with a sense of love, community, and sincere kindness than trying to steamroll people into belief. Believing in God, relating to God, having a relationship with Him can't be forced. It's something people either believe in and desire to have, or they do not, and we cannot think our persuasiveness with words is what draws people to God. God draws people to God, and we can also draw people to God by His method – loving kindness – if we are willing to put it into practice.

Goodness

There are three subheadings in the English translation of *hesed*: goodness, kindness, and faithfulness. Goodness is one of those terms that gets thrown around a lot, but I think we don't really understand just what it means and how it should impact our lives. "Goodness" in the true Biblical sense of the word is more than just not being bad. It is about exemplifying certain aspects of God's character as our own, and about being upright in our hearts and lives. As people, our actions of goodness reflect in our personal uprightness, and sees our way fit to imitate God, just as children imitate their parents.

This means goodness is something that we learn from God and we desire to imitate in our own lives, reflecting God's goodness to others through our own actions. In goodness, we recognize that certain things aren't right, nor proper, for us to do, and we refrain from doing them. But instead of looking at goodness as a big, long "don't" list, it is really about becoming something other than what we might start out as in the natural. Instead of behaving any which despicable way, offending others and leading both us and others into sin, goodness calls us on the carpet for whatever we are doing that is contrary to the nature we now have in Christ.

YES, YOU WHO TRUST HIM RECOGNIZE THE HONOR GOD HAS GIVEN HIM. BUT FOR THOSE WHO REJECT HIM,

"THE STONE THAT THE BUILDERS REJECTED
HAS NOW BECOME THE CORNERSTONE."

AND,

Dr. Lee Ann B. Marino, Ph.D., D.Min., D.D.

"HE IS THE STONE THAT MAKES PEOPLE STUMBLE, THE ROCK THAT MAKES THEM FALL."

THEY STUMBLE BECAUSE THEY DO NOT OBEY GOD'S WORD, AND SO THEY MEET THE FATE THAT WAS PLANNED FOR THEM.

BUT YOU ARE NOT LIKE THAT, FOR YOU ARE A CHOSEN PEOPLE. YOU ARE ROYAL PRIESTS, A HOLY NATION, GOD'S VERY OWN POSSESSION. AS A RESULT, YOU CAN SHOW OTHERS THE GOODNESS OF GOD, FOR HE CALLED YOU OUT OF THE DARKNESS INTO HIS WONDERFUL LIGHT.

"ONCE YOU HAD NO IDENTITY AS A PEOPLE;
  NOW YOU ARE GOD'S PEOPLE.
ONCE YOU RECEIVED NO MERCY;
  NOW YOU HAVE RECEIVED GOD'S MERCY."

DEAR FRIENDS, I WARN YOU AS "TEMPORARY RESIDENTS AND FOREIGNERS" TO KEEP AWAY FROM WORLDLY DESIRES THAT WAGE WAR AGAINST YOUR VERY SOULS. BE CAREFUL TO LIVE PROPERLY AMONG YOUR UNBELIEVING NEIGHBORS. THEN EVEN IF THEY ACCUSE YOU OF DOING WRONG, THEY WILL SEE YOUR HONORABLE BEHAVIOR, AND THEY WILL GIVE HONOR TO GOD WHEN HE JUDGES THE WORLD. (1 Peter 2:7-12)

This particular passage of Scripture contrasts the work of goodness with the work of our former lives, and it proves that such is evidence of a transformation from darkness to light. At one point in time, all of us lived however we wanted. We didn't emulate God, but we emulated the works of darkness. Even if we "weren't that bad" by the standards society tends to judge us by, we still missed the mark when it came to sin and did something, somewhere, that we shouldn't have in light of spirituality. Now that we have this opportunity to become something new through Christ, goodness is our aspiration. It's clearly rooted in the love of God, because as we love God, our urge to do something good isn't just for one person or just to make sure we all look good in the eyes of someone else. It prompts us to make sure our actions line up with our new beliefs, our new life, and most importantly, whatever it is we claim to believe.

That's what goodness is; it's an aligner. Goodness calls us to be more than we were yesterday and to walk in everything we know is right, right now. Even if we don't have something specific to do for someone else, goodness reminds us that doing right is about our behavior, in and out, even when no one else is looking. It is the love of God stirring us within to be different than we used to be and to make sure everything we do is a part of that change. We live and abide by dignity and respect for all, and become true evangelizers of the Gospel, even without saying a word.

Kindness

We have already talked about the concept of loving-kindness to a certain extent. We understand the "love" principle therein as we are close to and learning how to understand it better, and here we will specifically talk about what kindness is and how kindness impacts our world of love. In the last section, we talked about goodness and how as a quality, goodness calls our behavior to match our claims. We all have met Christians who claimed certain beliefs, but their general actions and outlook on life didn't seem to match those beliefs. We could stand from a mile away and see every which way things don't measure up, but the closer we got, it becomes obvious just how blurred their lines became. The discipline between principle and conviction, between living right and doing right often feel far more complicated than they might be. The answer lies in discovering our foundations, and in those foundations, embodying a sense of love in action.

That's how I define kindness, as love in action. When we love, it prompts us to do something, and the result is an outlook and action that is truly kind. We can't be kind and keep it to ourselves, so our urge to do something becomes so great, we desire to do more than just muse or have ideals about beliefs; we want to do something. When we are kind, our actions match our beliefs: we refrain from passing judgment on others, we live by truth, we live repentant lives, we refrain from being stubborn or unrepentant, and we seek to do good, in any and every situation.

YOU MAY THINK YOU CAN CONDEMN SUCH PEOPLE, BUT YOU ARE JUST AS BAD, AND YOU HAVE NO EXCUSE! WHEN YOU SAY THEY ARE WICKED AND SHOULD BE PUNISHED, YOU ARE CONDEMNING YOURSELF, FOR YOU WHO JUDGE OTHERS DO THESE VERY SAME THINGS. AND WE KNOW THAT GOD, IN HIS JUSTICE, WILL PUNISH

ANYONE WHO DOES SUCH THINGS. SINCE YOU JUDGE OTHERS FOR DOING THESE THINGS, WHY DO YOU THINK YOU CAN AVOID GOD'S JUDGMENT WHEN YOU DO THE SAME THINGS? DON'T YOU SEE HOW WONDERFULLY KIND, TOLERANT, AND PATIENT GOD IS WITH YOU? DOES THIS MEAN NOTHING TO YOU? CAN'T YOU SEE THAT HIS KINDNESS IS INTENDED TO TURN YOU FROM YOUR SIN? (Romans 2:1-4)

The "agenda" of kindness is to turn away from sin and toward something better: the goodness of God. Instead of leading people to stumble or find an implausible, impossible way to follow, kindness helps others along by pushing them to do right, extending a sense of warmth and love toward others, and avoiding the temptation to let others stumble. We can't escape the reality that the world we live in is selfish, people consider their own wants and needs first and want to do for themselves. Kindness reminds us that not everything is about us, and that in kindness, we must open our hearts to offer to others and behave in a manner that seeks to make people better, rather than more isolated and alienated.

Kindness opens up the world to others in ways that are ordinary and every day: offering someone a cup of coffee, a listening ear, giving an offering to a ministry in need, providing a good meal to someone, a word in due season, a gift for no particular reason, offering to do something without charge or limitation, and just a great sense of being able to give to others as giving something deeper to them than a thing or object. In kindness, we don't just do; we give love from the heart of God through us to someone else.

Faithfulness

If goodness is something that aligns us to love and kindness is love in action, then faithfulness is the condition and action of our faith, present to make us people who live lives that reflect faith. If we are people who believe that God is love, that means love is something we come to believe in, something that is an essential part of our faith. We meet so many in this world who say they don't believe in love, and they don't believe that love is real, and such is the tragedy created by a lack of faithfulness in their lives. When people are faithless, the result is a lack of love, and that lack of love makes people question their very faith. When we are faith-full, or full of our faith and walking out that state in our lives, there is no question that faith – and therefore, love is real.

Faithfulness is about a lot more than just being of good reputation, being around others, or the condition of being loyal in one's life. There is no question that such things are good and important, but faithfulness is having the ability to remain in faith and stay committed toward all the things of faith that we believe are real and true, even if we don't see those things right now in our lives. It is the ultimate promise, hope, and realization that God is love and love is, therefore real, because we know that God is a part of our lives, and we are a part of His heart. In faithfulness, we are operating on faith, not needing immediate results to manifest, pleasing God, reaping a reward by faith, believing for the impossible, and accepting the fact that we are different from others in this life. Because we are faithful, we have come to deal with the fact that what we believe for, hope for, and offer to this world is different and that it is all right to be different in that way. Our God Himself is faithful to us, showing us a different, reliable way, and helping us to offer that way in this difficult world.

UNFAILING LOVE AND FAITHFULNESS MAKE ATONEMENT FOR SIN. BY FEARING THE LORD, PEOPLE AVOID EVIL. (Proverbs 16:6)

Faithfulness opens the door for repentance, but it does it through love, which is an interesting facet. When repentance comes about through faithfulness, it establishes a foundation for people to build a spiritual life upon. Rather than running in and tearing everything down, it lays down the possibility for something new to be built. Faithfulness gives an opportunity to live an entirely new life, that new life of faith we are always talking about. If we are willing to be faithful, God will change our ordinary to extraordinary, every single time.

Love stirred to action

Hesed is the ultimate connection between what we feel and are stirred to do. We can't claim to be Christians and not react in our faith without a sense of practical love. *Hesed* provides us that practical outlet of kindness, goodness, and faithfulness, all with the intent to share what we have learned from God Himself. Our faith must have character and so must our love. If we make love nothing more than a distant, out-there, strange musing, it doesn't manifest in such a way that others can relate and embrace it for themselves. It is God's will that all we do in Him is accessible, and as we grow in love that stirs us to do for others, we see His love manifest in a more practical way.

FOR THY LOVINGKINDNESS IS BEFORE MINE EYES: AND I HAVE WALKED IN THY TRUTH. (Psalm 26:3)

Yes, we must feel that stirring, allowing ourselves to hear the calling of the Holy Spirit to a greater walk of love and greater deeds. No longer shall we be people who claim to love and fail to apply action; we shall be those who can be recognizable, because as Christians, they shall know us by our love.

Reflections

- How is love both a "feeling" and an action?

- Why is it important to see our love manifest in deeds?

- How do we reconcile the battle of faith and works with love?

- How does God draw us to Himself?

- What do goodness, kindness, and faithfulness teach us about love?

Chapter Four

FRIENDSHIP (*RAHAM* AND *PHILEO*)

Raham[1]
רָחַם racham {raw-kham'}

Meanings:
- to love
- love deeply
- have mercy
- be compassionate
- have tender affection
- have compassion
- of God
- or man
- to be shown compassion

Phileo[2]
φιλαδελφία, ας, ἡ philadelphia {fil-ad-el-fee'-ah}

Meanings:
- love of brothers or sisters
- brotherly love
- in the NT the love which Christians cherish for each other as brethren

Dr. Lee Ann B. Marino, Ph.D., D.Min., D.D.

CHURCHES are notorious for preaching about marriage, families, and sometimes church relationships. We can almost recite the advice, perspectives, and yes, lectures on familial and church interactions. The advice is the same, but there is often gaps in the understandings of those interpersonal relationships: we aren't told exactly how to get from point A to point B in them. We are told that spouses should love one another and should love their children and we are told that we should love others in the church, but what does any of that mean? How do we love those we don't like, and how do we distinguish between the two? And what does any of this have to do with what we are discussing in this chapter?

This chapter is a front and center look at a specific aspect of love that often overlaps into other relations and makes us all better: friendship. Learning about friendship, how friendship makes us better, and how we can be better friends to others is all a process in learning about the choices we make in love to those who are closest to us. This chapter is all about the family we choose (and learning how to sometimes love our own families even better): here's to friendship, the perfect blendship, and the perfect opportunity to love people in a different way to enhance the overall quality of human experience.

Properly defining raham and phileo

Raham and *phileo* aren't words in great debate. They are consistently defined as words to describe specific affection toward someone, which reflects the characteristics and importance of friendship. More than just expounding on friendship, however, both *raham* and *phileo* often go to depths to describe friendship in their definitions. They express friendship as a loving kinship; so much so, it is described as a brotherly love. Within its parameters, you find deep love, mercy, compassionate, genuine affection, and the showing of these different attributes (especially compassion) as it is exercised and experienced. In *raham* and *phileo* we find the fullness of the choice of love among humans (and even with God), choosing to love and embrace our friends closely, knowing we like who they are, and believe the best for them as they believe the best for us.

The uniqueness of friendship

Friendship is a very special thing in this world. Those who have friends recognize there is just not quite anything else like it. No matter how old or young we are or where we come from in this world, we all gravitate toward our friends, spending time with them and experiencing life with them. Friends of all sorts enrich our world, adding color and dimension whereby we might not experience things or learn what we do, all thanks to them.

Friendship reminds us that the world is full of good people: those who are different from us as well as those who are like us. In a way we might not always understand, it helps us to be less afraid of the world, of the unknown and of those that we have not met quite yet. Unlike familial love, which is exclusive, the love of *raham* and *phileo* extends our borders and our world, introducing us to a whole new realm of love and involvement with others outside of our immediate families. We are welcomed into a new form of family, of living and interacting, and dealing with the ups and downs of human nature that are sometimes a blessing and sometimes difficult. As we learn about human support, we come into a place where we are a little more trusting and a little bit better, just because we have experienced the love of friendship.

THERE ARE "FRIENDS" WHO DESTROY EACH OTHER, BUT A REAL FRIEND STICKS CLOSER THAN A BROTHER. (Proverbs 18:24)

The Scriptures reveal to us the fullness of friendship: the way that it provides us with a whole new sense of loyalty and recognizes that there are trustworthy people in this world, outside of our families, who we can rely on in times of trouble, need, and in good times, as well. They will be the people who stick with us, closer sometimes than our own families, reminding us that the world is bigger than those to whom we are related. It is not God's will for us that we should be afraid of the world. We are here to fellowship, to love one another, to support each other, and to come to a greater understanding in the mutual worship of God. It is God's desire we do that not just on our own, but with others, as well. In distorted situations forged by dysfunctional family alliances, it's easy for us to be afraid of anyone who is outside of or different from us. Modern-day politics and news headlines don't help. They make us believe that people in other places are so different from us, there is no way we could have anything in common with them. As we shut the world out, we fail to see potential, unmet friends, and develop walls and hostilities that keep us from exploring the incredible beauty and love present in humanity.

Friendship is unique because it demands its own loyalties and alliances for no reason at all except two people have forged a bond that might seem otherwise unlikely. Friendship seldom makes sense in a literal sense, it comes and goes and just rests there between people because it is created by God. In bonding and creating friendships with others we also learn about the friendship we have with God, as believers. This makes friendship special, because it touches the heart of humanity as well as our experience with divinity, and teaches us valuable lessons about loyalty, interacting with others, and recognizing love stands unique in our lives as we learn to like the world around us (and those who happen to be in it).

A progression of love

One thing I've noticed as I have taken the time to research for this book is the way that the different forms of love build on each other. I believe God reveals to us about these different expressions of love so we will ultimately find Him and His love as we continue to pursue it.

To properly understand friendship, we have to see the different forms of love coming together to create what is often called friendship or sometimes "brotherly love." With friends, we are drawn to them – a drawing or attraction, of sorts. It isn't romantic in nature, but neither is the exclusive understanding of such a term for love, either. We form an alliance with our friends, not unlike that which we form with our families. We agree to be there for one another and care for one another, and we set up a relationship that we don't just have with everybody we encounter. Then, hopefully a sense of loving-kindness is present in our relationships with our friends. Our inclination toward them causes us to express our care and concern for them with action, and that means we spend time with our friends, do things for them, and also have them do things for us. It is an entire merging of the forms of love we have studied up to this point, now manifesting in people who are not necessarily our blood relatives, necessarily of our clan, or having anything to do with our origins, whatsoever. They are people God has given us a heart for, a love for, and a bond with, combining and helping us to grow and expand our love beyond that which seems immediate or most accessible.

NEVER ABANDON A FRIEND— EITHER YOURS OR YOUR FATHER'S. WHEN DISASTER STRIKES, YOU WON'T HAVE TO ASK YOUR BROTHER FOR ASSISTANCE. IT'S BETTER TO GO TO A NEIGHBOR THAN TO A BROTHER WHO LIVES FAR AWAY. (Proverbs 27:10)

Our friends teach us about entirely new levels of love within our lives and personal capabilities. There are many people who speak of loving someone but not being "in love" with them – these people are talking about a strong and abiding friendship that has a platonic characteristic to it. From this description, we can actually understand a lot about friendship and the kind of love it embodies. Friendship is a non-romantic love that can be just as strong and committed without a sexual component. We can love and honor our friends as much as we do any marriage. Friendship is also associated outside of families, although sometimes people (in modern times) have forged close friendships and relationships with their relatives. The difference is that they aren't aligned with their relatives because they are their relatives; they are aligned out of a sense of friendship, of loving and liking their family members for who they are as people, rather than as being a part of one family.

For us to say we have friends or are friends, these different components must be present. We must be, and express, an appreciation for who we all are. We must like our friends, as opposed to just loving them – and we will understand this differentiation a little later on. We must do for our friends, and they must do for us. We shouldn't fear our friends or find fear present in our interaction. Our friends help us see and embrace things differently, being less intimidated by those we don't know, and coming to see we have things in common with others we have met and have yet to meet. Friendship gives us a sense of satisfaction in love, of loving and being loved back, just for who we are, and inspires us to keep connected and hopeful that love will continue to transform life as we are willing to reach out to take and experience it.

Types of friends

The Bible doesn't make many distinctions between social acquaintances, occasional friends, work friends, church friends, school friends, close friends, and best friends as we often do today. In Biblical times, people didn't have so many friends they had to distinguish between all of them and assign each of them a distinct role in one's life. They had their families, a few people they might have met in their local cities, and that was about it in the friendship department. People didn't have the ease of social media or other communication avenues to keep in contact with people who were far away. This means that friends were very important to people, especially when an individual or group was far from their native home and the rest of their familial kinship. Forging bonds outside of family members was often necessary for survival and continuance and growing to find that you could trust people outside of your immediate clan became a huge asset in the struggle to live. Friends were friends were friends, and the more one developed bonds with friends, the more they learned about the goodness present in the world around them.

The major distinction the Bible makes among friends is between good friends – those who are loyal with you – and bad friends, or those who are not loyal, or somehow corrupt otherwise good character. For this very reason the Bible encourages us to be very careful of those we associate with, those we take into our hearts as friends, and to use good judgement with those we are closest to in this life.

THEY VISIT ME AS IF THEY WERE MY FRIENDS, BUT ALL THE WHILE THEY GATHER GOSSIP, AND WHEN THEY LEAVE, THEY SPREAD IT EVERYWHERE. (Psalm 41:6)

AS FOR MY COMPANION, HE BETRAYED HIS FRIENDS; HE BROKE HIS PROMISES. (Psalm 55:20)

WITH THEIR WORDS, THE GODLESS DESTROY THEIR FRIENDS, BUT KNOWLEDGE WILL RESCUE THE RIGHTEOUS. (Proverbs 11:9)

The gift of discernment is very useful when it comes to our friendships because we must make sure we pursue our friends for the right reasons, keeping it safe and godly for all involved. Even though friendship is placed within us by God, that doesn't mean we always pursue relationships that are good for us. It's possible to want specific friends because they will improve our social circle or elevate us in some way. It's also possible to want certain friends for certain favors or exchanges with the "right" kind of people. We can misuse and abuse others in friendship as easily as they can do so to us, and that means our friends and friendships should be something that seeks to be a blessing and uphold the path we know we are called to be on (as well as edify the paths of others). No matter how close we might be to our friends, friendship should focus on mutual edification, and everyone involved should be better for it.

The difference between love and like

You've got an endless number of people who will debate the difference between love vs. like on social media. If you don't believe me, try it sometime. Make a comment to the extent that "God commands us to love – not like – others." See what people say. You will, most likely, get a series of "amen!" choruses followed by people who start an argument over what exactly the difference is. Yes, it's completely true that God has told us to love others, not like them, but the naysayers have a point: what is the difference between love and like?

In love, the difference between the two is a divine love of discipline, a familial love of obligation, or a friendship love out of choice and interest. What this means in simpler terms: the difference between love and like is what draws us to people, and in friendship we choose our friends because something about them draws them to us. We like our friends; we don't just love them. They are a choice that we make, because something in who they are is pleasing to us.

We don't get to choose our family. In Biblical times, people didn't get to choose their marital partners, either. Everything was arranged by family members or a strange sense of fate, all with the intention of personal growth and the integrity of societal structures. These people might have grown to have some sense of love in the ways we have already spoken of – they might feel aligned or obliged to others, and they might even have some form of physical attraction – but that doesn't mean they genuinely ever like one another as people, for who they are.

This hits home at the difference between love and like: when we like someone, we embrace who they are as a person and enjoy them for that reason. We aren't forced to be with them or to remain with them out of any sort of requirement. Friends are friends, are friends: they are the ones we choose, the ones we run to, the ones we explore our lives and the world with, those we both support and find support and comfort in, and those we want to be with, just because we do. We like them in addition to loving them, and this makes all the difference in our every relationship.

"OR SUPPOSE A WOMAN HAS TEN SILVER COINS AND LOSES ONE. WON'T SHE LIGHT A LAMP AND SWEEP THE ENTIRE HOUSE AND SEARCH CAREFULLY UNTIL SHE FINDS IT? AND WHEN SHE FINDS IT, SHE WILL CALL IN HER FRIENDS AND NEIGHBORS AND SAY, 'REJOICE WITH ME BECAUSE I HAVE FOUND MY LOST COIN.' IN THE SAME WAY, THERE IS JOY IN THE PRESENCE OF GOD'S ANGELS WHEN EVEN ONE SINNER REPENTS." (Luke 15:8-10)

To most of us reading this parable, the idea of a woman calling up her friends over a lost coin and expecting them to care might sound strange. There is a truth in it, however, about love and like combined present in it. The woman's friends knew how important finding the coin was to her, and they rejoiced in her victory. It is the same for us: any time we call up our friends about something that's important to us, or they call us up with something important to them. We are celebrating our friends, offering something to them that we care about them, and what matters in their lives, even if no one else does. Thus, friendship is almost an easy form of love: it is easy to talk to our friends, to forgive their wrongdoings, to be forgiven, to spend time together, and to enjoy each other. It's why we run to our friends rather than judgmental family members and sometimes confide far more in our friends than in our spouses. Our friends connect with us on a "like" level, and it makes them easy for us to love. We can celebrate them and look to them for a sense of acceptance that is often missing in other parts of our lives.

Finding love right where we are

One of my favorite episodes of the show *Friends* is titled "The One with the Two Parties." For Rachel's birthday, Monica throws a birthday party that quickly gets disrupted because Rachel's parents show up, who are involved in a bitter and nasty divorce at the time. In an effort to avoid ruining her entire birthday, the group takes on two parties, aiming to keep her parents apart. They deal with broken furniture, people trying to sneak out of Monica's boring party to go to Joey and Chandler's lively and raucous party across the hall, Ross running back and forth to keep Rachel's father out of the other party where her mother was, Joey kissing Monica's mother to keep her from seeing Rachel's father, and the guys making general idiots of themselves, all to make sure Rachel can divide her time between the two parents without one parent knowing the other one was at the party.

One of the best scenes was a discussion between Chandler and Rachel. Chandler was able to sit down and talk to Rachel about having divorced parents because his parents divorced when he was a young child. They sat and sorted things out, and through the commonality, Chandler gave Rachel something that she might not otherwise have found.

Rachel and Chandler never dated during the series. They were never more than friends who supported and cared about each other, got into occasional trouble together, and enjoyed having fun with each other. Even though Ross and Rachel were dating at this point in the series, the person Rachel needed to talk to was Chandler, not Ross, and Ross understood that. He didn't get jealous, accuse Rachel of having an affair, or get angry at her because he knew who she was and what she needed, he couldn't offer her at that moment. Chandler was a friend, able to help Rachel with what she was going through because he had been there. While Ross might have empathized, cared, even been attentive to her situation, he wasn't going to be able to give her what she needed at that moment.

A FRIEND IS ALWAYS LOYAL, AND A BROTHER IS BORN TO HELP IN TIME OF NEED. (Proverbs 17:17)

What Rachel experienced is what I call the "maybe we found love right where we are" effect. Rachel had someone around her who knew and understood enough to love her through it. It didn't just fall on one person or mate to help her, because at that time her mate couldn't offer what was needed. Contrary to popular belief, we do need more people in our lives than just a formal mate or spouse. A spouse can't always be our friend, and we can't expect that one person is able to love us the right way, all the time. Friends offer us that sense of finding love wherever we are, and it touches us in a way that helps us get through some of the most difficult times we may experience. When people are lonely and often think they are lonely for a relationship, what they are really missing is the feeling of finding love where they are, among their friends. There's something comforting about experiencing a circle of love and knowing you are loved beyond those you are closest to or experience in your immediate family or circumstances. It helps to remind you that you are never alone, and that in never being alone, love permeates and transcends your experience, right where you are.

Friendship misconceptions

Most of us have seen the movie *Grease*, featuring the final musical number at the end of the carnival scene. The characters (all high school students) pledge their eternal loyalty to one another as they belt out the words, "We'll always be together." It fills us with warm fuzzies because it reminds us of what life was like at high school age and how we all genuinely believed that we would be together forever, joined and bound at the hip, always having the same things in common and the same interests. The realities we found, however, are that we no longer have many of the friends we had in high school (or junior high, or as children, or even in college). Even if we have managed to keep in contact with them, our relationships are often no longer the same. We aren't as close, life has caused us to take a different interest in those we know or those who are around us, and our life changes have altered our interests and perceptions in what is important and what we look for in our friends and support systems.

THE GODLY GIVE GOOD ADVICE TO THEIR FRIENDS; THE WICKED LEAD THEM ASTRAY. (Proverbs 12:26)

It's important to realize that there are many things about friendship that have a way of changing over time, and that not every image or concept we see about friendship in the world is always accurate. I do believe our entertainment images of friendship leave us unprepared for the ups and downs we will experience among our friends in this life. There will be people who once were our friends who will leave us high and dry, there will be those who we thought were our friends but never were, there are those who will be friends for a season and we will drift apart or lose touch, and there will be those who we will end our friendships with on a sour note, and there will be those who we no longer find we have much in common with anymore. Friends come and go and relationships with others change, and there is nothing wrong with this. What is wrong is when we get so hung up on a person or a relationship that we find ourselves unable to move forward. It is certainly understandable to be sad and to miss our friends, but we can't be people who live in what was or what won't ever be again, because such positioning keeps us from meeting new friends and opening ourselves up to a whole new world.

It's also important to recognize that friendship changes with time. Sometimes we are close to one person for a while and then we are close to someone else, without abandoning a friendship all together. As we grow through life, our friendship needs may easily change. Our faith has a way of taking us from one set of priorities to another, and that means the ones who are around us and closest to us also change. Whether it's getting married, divorced, having kids, accepting a ministry call, moving away, or stepping up to join a new ministry or unleashing a new step in one's life, our friendships must adjust to where we are going versus where we have always been.

As we grow in our faith, we also come to learn that some people just aren't who we always thought they were (or maybe it's nothing more than we aren't who we used to be). The things that once drew us close to people don't always last long-term, and sometimes we come to see a side of people that is disconcerting enough to cause distance or disconnection. Discernment helps us to know who is for us and who isn't, how we can be a good friend to those who are around us, and how to best handle each and every situation with friends, whether it is connection or disconnection.

In the same thought, friendship isn't all about having people who just encourage you no matter what you desire to do. Sometimes I think we get the idea that we should never disagree with our friends and that they should never intervene if we are doing something wrong, stupid, or just heading in a dangerous direction. There are times when our friends offer guidance and they are wrong, but true friends genuinely care about us and are concerned when it seems like we are going in a bad direction or one that doesn't seem to make a lot of sense. Our friends should be there to spark interest, to make us think about the things we undertake, and to help us see the world from a new angle. Any time a friend is always there with approval rather than some challenge from time to time should cause us to wonder how honest they are with us.

Friendship requires something of everyone involved in its participation, so never assume that it's all about everyone else or all about you. It's about both of you, about everyone who is a part of such a friendship, and that means friendship requires some time out of us all. If you want to be a good friend and want good friends, put in the time and experience the time put in to create an entire relationship.

Friendships don't always last, but the good news about friendship is the world is full of unmet friends and individuals who are looking for good people to meet and good friends to know. Yes, one friend might not work out, but someone else is out there, waiting and ready to meet you.

When friends become family

Not too long ago I met someone who instantly became my "friend as family." It wasn't something I could easily describe, because it never is. It was just that instant, immediate connection, one that bounded with that promise of becoming something more than just a friend, but not a lover. It was that sense of familial love, present between people who didn't know each other biologically and for all respective stories, couldn't have been more different.

THERE ARE "FRIENDS" WHO DESTROY EACH OTHER, BUT A REAL FRIEND STICKS CLOSER THAN A BROTHER. (Proverbs 18:24)

We have already examined the experiences of Naomi and Ruth and David and Jonathan in friendship, because they were friends who became as family. In both instances, Ruth and Jonathan placed Naomi and David above their own relatives, which was highly uncommon at such a time in history. These individuals experienced something many of us will come to experience in our lifetimes: that of experiencing a friend who is more like family to you than just a friend, someone who is a part of your life, your kinship, if you will, beyond just a mere acquaintance or someone you spend some time with on occasion.

We can echo the realities of Naomi and Ruth and David and Jonathan for inspiration in what it looks like when we have friends who become like family to us:

- We love each other beyond just a casual love that many have for their friends. It is a true and abiding love; shown through the actions we extend to one another. There is no mere lip service here, but real action to display true friendship!

- We have a commitment, or covenant, with them. It's not as formal as signing a document, but as real as expressions through the things we say, and we do.

- They are there for us and we are there for them, even if it costs us something.

- We can trust their guidance because we know they have our best interests at heart.

- Even though we do not always disagree, we have learned how to respect differences, walk in forgiveness, and reconcile occasional pains.

- We know and recognize they are not there to take advantage of us, nor are we there to take advantage of them.

- The interaction and expression are just as if we were biologically related, and there is no distinction made that we are not really biologically family.

- We care about their families as much as we care about our own families. We commit to be there with them throughout their lives, even in the wake of someone's death.

These are friends we should truly love and hold fast to in our lives. While yes, sometimes friendships change and these associations change as well, friends who become family are an anchor in the way we experience the world. When our families fail us and the world grows cold, it is those who love us as much as any relative should who help us to get through and to restore our faith that humanity can be just in some way again. These friends remind us that love is real and love is bigger than just those we might know immediately. Love is bigger and beyond anything we might experience biologically; it is a true experience that transcends.

What kind of friend are you?

The modern-day headlines of pastors committing suicide, driven to a seeming state of despair and hopelessness, inspires grief in many, judgment in some, and questioning in all. It doesn't seem to make sense to us that leaders who speak on the love of God could ever find themselves in such a state as to end their lives. As more and more information comes out about the situations, however, we learn of deep, long states of depression, despair, and hopelessness that have often set in. They feel overworked, underappreciated, and sometimes, even unloved.

One of the common themes I have noted between ministers who have committed suicide and ministers I've dealt with who are depressed or unhappy is the lack of friendship in their lives. Because they are ministers, they often find themselves disconnected from others. Having to be a leader means that you don't go running to your congregations with every little problem and between betrayals and false friends, many church leaders have serious trust issues. The result is a state of loneliness: leaders who are very alone and isolated, distant and afraid to trust others. This means they don't have the connections of friendship to help catch them when they are down, feeling unloved, or feeling overworked.

Someone might argue, "Well they have their families!" but this isn't the same as the love among friends, and family members don't always understand, nor empathize, with the difficulties church leaders experience. There is nothing wrong with families and familial support but expecting a minister's spouse and children to catch all the problems, needs, and issues that a minister may have in their unique experience is unrealistic. Somewhere, at some point in time, a minister needs true, comprehensive friends they can rely on. Instead of having people who come to them all the time with a need, ministers need people who they can go to in the experience of friendship sometimes, as well.

In other words, ministers are feeling deep hopelessness and despair because they just don't have the right kind of friends in their lives. They are used to being sources of hope, inspiration, and helping people through their problems, but they have a hard time finding people who will do the same for them. It causes these people to feel alone and hopeless, like nobody really loves them for who they are as people.

This isn't to say their feelings are reasonable or realistic. I haven't a single doubt that there are many kind and sincere people who seek to do right by ministers and who care about them. Somewhere in their struggles, however, that is the message they've gotten, whether deliberate or unintentional. The messages we send to others tell them a lot, and people aren't quick to miss how we feel about them. Yet their struggles should demand a question of all of us: what kind of friends are we? Do our friends know how we feel about them, and are there ways we can be better friends?

If we are going to talk about friendship in love, we must also talk about the kind of friend we are and seek to be. It's great to hope and desire to have good friends, but one of the reasons we are often not very close to others is because we seek to have friends who are a specific way toward us, but we don't focus on how we treat other people. If we want to be good friends, how we treat our friends is just as important as how they treat us.

UNFRIENDLY PEOPLE CARE ONLY ABOUT THEMSELVES;
   THEY LASH OUT AT COMMON SENSE. (Proverbs 18:1)

A MAN THAT HATH FRIENDS MUST SHEW HIMSELF FRIENDLY: AND THERE IS A FRIEND THAT STICKETH CLOSER THAN A BROTHER. (Proverbs 18:24, KJV)

MANY WILL SAY THEY ARE LOYAL FRIENDS, BUT WHO CAN FIND ONE WHO IS TRULY RELIABLE? (Proverbs 20:6)

Even though we might want people in our lives, we can easily convey a message to others that tells them we don't want them around, we don't welcome new people, and we don't want to be bothered. Think about it for a minute. Much of what we proclaim on social media is how much we don't need anyone else. We don't care what others think of us, or what their opinions might be. We state how it's only God that matters to us. This is often not the case, but have we considered what that says to others about who we are and what we are doing? Those posts may very well be someone's first impression of someone else, and they send a message that they aren't interested in connecting to other people. This might seem like an issue reserved to social media, but the reality is that we can give those same messages to people with our attitudes, the way we express our opinions, our body language, and our perceptions can all convey something that doesn't say, "I'm loving and friendly!"

There are also many who might claim to have friends but are not loyal or devoted to them. They never call or communicate, they are forever borrowing money and not paying it back, always taking without giving, and always putting their own needs and priorities above their friends. This is an instance where someone is lucky to have good friends, but is taking advantage of them. Yes, we all go through different times and experiences in our lives where sometimes our friends give more than we do, but that shouldn't be the consistent, never-ending case in a relationship. We need to give and be there for our friends, with the same expectation as they are there for us. Just as we expect others to be good friends, we must be them, too.

Friendship is a discipline. It forces us to love in action, not just in word, but in real deed. If you want friends, be friendly. Express your love as a human being for others. Make it known that you are a dedicated person and have the ability to be a loyal friend. Be someone that others desire to be around and select people who want to be around you. To have good friends, be a good friend!

When friendship goes awry

It's not the most fun thing to deal with, but sometimes friendships go awry. There can be any number of ways that it happens, but when we hit the wall with our friends, it can be hard to pick up and dust off to start over again. The reason it's hard is because as was stated earlier, friendship is our open window to the world. It is our immediate venture out into the world to experience other people beyond those we deem as close or as safe. Yet sometimes, we run into negative encounters with our friends. We can think they are there for us and will stand with us through hard times, and discover something else, all together.

WHEN THREE OF JOB'S FRIENDS HEARD OF THE TRAGEDY HE HAD SUFFERED, THEY GOT TOGETHER AND TRAVELED FROM THEIR HOMES TO COMFORT AND CONSOLE HIM. THEIR NAMES WERE ELIPHAZ THE TEMANITE, BILDAD THE SHUHITE, AND ZOPHAR THE NAAMATHITE. WHEN THEY SAW JOB FROM A DISTANCE, THEY SCARCELY RECOGNIZED HIM. WAILING LOUDLY, THEY TORE THEIR ROBES AND THREW DUST INTO THE AIR OVER THEIR HEADS TO SHOW THEIR GRIEF. THEN THEY SAT ON THE GROUND WITH HIM FOR SEVEN DAYS AND NIGHTS. NO ONE SAID A WORD TO JOB, FOR THEY SAW THAT HIS SUFFERING WAS TOO GREAT FOR WORDS. (Job 2:11-13)

We've all heard teaching about Job's friends. They certainly weren't a bunch of friends you'd want to get stranded with on a desert island somewhere, because it's obvious you wouldn't survive. Job was down and out, and we sat back and wondered, why did Job ever consider them to be friends to begin with? Well, the answer to that is found in Job 2:11-13, even though we don't see it. We focus on the results of Job's specific encounters with his friends during his trial, but it's obvious from this passage that they weren't always so unhelpful. They were called "Job's friends" because there was a time when they were his friends: they shared their lives together, they went through things together, they encouraged each other, they knew each other, and they experienced things together. They didn't start out as problems or enemies, and they weren't always so unsupportive of Job.

The words he went on to say to his friends don't sound very friendly, however.

ONE SHOULD BE KIND TO A FAINTING FRIEND,
BUT YOU ACCUSE ME WITHOUT ANY FEAR OF THE ALMIGHTY.
MY BROTHERS, YOU HAVE PROVED AS UNRELIABLE AS A SEASONAL BROOK
THAT OVERFLOWS ITS BANKS IN THE SPRING
WHEN IT IS SWOLLEN WITH ICE AND MELTING SNOW.
BUT WHEN THE HOT WEATHER ARRIVES, THE WATER DISAPPEARS.
THE BROOK VANISHES IN THE HEAT.
THE CARAVANS TURN ASIDE TO BE REFRESHED,
BUT THERE IS NOTHING TO DRINK, SO THEY DIE.
THE CARAVANS FROM TEMA SEARCH FOR THIS WATER;
THE TRAVELERS FROM SHEBA HOPE TO FIND IT.
THEY COUNT ON IT BUT ARE DISAPPOINTED.
WHEN THEY ARRIVE, THEIR HOPES ARE DASHED.
YOU, TOO, HAVE GIVEN NO HELP.
YOU HAVE SEEN MY CALAMITY, AND YOU ARE AFRAID.
BUT WHY? HAVE I EVER ASKED YOU FOR A GIFT?
HAVE I BEGGED FOR ANYTHING OF YOURS FOR

MYSELF?
HAVE I ASKED YOU TO RESCUE ME FROM MY ENEMIES,
    OR TO SAVE ME FROM RUTHLESS PEOPLE?
TEACH ME, AND I WILL KEEP QUIET.
    SHOW ME WHAT I HAVE DONE WRONG.
HONEST WORDS CAN BE PAINFUL,
    BUT WHAT DO YOUR CRITICISMS AMOUNT TO?
DO YOU THINK YOUR WORDS ARE CONVINCING
    WHEN YOU DISREGARD MY CRY OF DESPERATION?
YOU WOULD EVEN SEND AN ORPHAN INTO SLAVERY
    OR SELL A FRIEND.
LOOK AT ME!
    WOULD I LIE TO YOUR FACE?
STOP ASSUMING MY GUILT,
    FOR I HAVE DONE NO WRONG.
DO YOU THINK I AM LYING?
    DON'T I KNOW THE DIFFERENCE BETWEEN RIGHT AND WRONG? (Job 6:14-30)

Job went through an experience that took him through a whole new dimension of life and analyzing life, and it wasn't something that others around him understood well. He went through something that his friends were just not ready to handle, and the change in Job was so notable, they didn't know how to handle it or him. Suddenly, nothing that they did together prior mattered in light of the way they were unable to stand with him through his trial. Friends are there to help you get through what you go through, and having the wrong people around can quickly make something worse. It's time to accept that sometimes those who've been with us can't go any further than they have gone, and it's important to release any offense and move toward the new season of life. New people will replace the old; it happens every time.

Friendship with God and in Christ

I think friendship is highly overlooked in church. We talk about God as our Father, we talk about us as being a family in Christ, but we don't often talk about the spiritual element of friendship in our walk with God and other believers. I think this is because sometimes we downplay the role of love in friendships and don't give it the credibility it deserves. Because friendship incorporates the principle of like, it can seem like friendship isn't a sacrifice that we make. As a result, we play up the sacrificial aspects of love while forgetting that friendship often involves a sense of sacrifice, unique to itself.

This hasn't always been the case, however. The group we more commonly call the Quakers actually have the formal title, the Society of Friends. They call themselves this to call attention to the Christian's friendship with God as well as their friendship with other believers. Being called "friends" emphasized their beliefs in a universal fellowship, the equality among believers, and their welcoming nature who sought God as they did. Being "friends" was a spiritual statement as well as a social one. By recognizing one another as friends, they laid aside class distinctions and racial and social designations to become one body, one group of believers transformed by Christ Jesus.

The Quakers realized something about themselves that all of us who are believers could benefit to learn: because we are believers, we are the friends of God and Christ, and as we are in Christ, we are friends with one another.

"I HAVE LOVED YOU EVEN AS THE FATHER HAS LOVED ME. REMAIN IN MY LOVE. WHEN YOU OBEY MY COMMANDMENTS, YOU REMAIN IN MY LOVE, JUST AS I OBEY MY FATHER'S COMMANDMENTS AND REMAIN IN HIS LOVE. I HAVE TOLD YOU THESE THINGS SO THAT YOU WILL BE FILLED WITH MY JOY. YES, YOUR JOY WILL OVERFLOW! THIS IS MY COMMANDMENT: LOVE EACH OTHER IN THE SAME WAY I HAVE LOVED YOU. THERE IS NO GREATER LOVE THAN TO LAY DOWN ONE'S LIFE FOR ONE'S FRIENDS. YOU ARE MY FRIENDS IF YOU DO WHAT I COMMAND. I NO LONGER CALL YOU SLAVES, BECAUSE A MASTER DOESN'T CONFIDE IN HIS SLAVES. NOW YOU ARE MY FRIENDS, SINCE I HAVE TOLD YOU EVERYTHING THE FATHER TOLD ME. YOU DIDN'T CHOOSE ME. I CHOSE YOU. I APPOINTED YOU TO GO AND PRODUCE LASTING FRUIT, SO THAT THE FATHER WILL GIVE YOU WHATEVER YOU ASK FOR, USING MY NAME. THIS IS MY COMMAND: LOVE EACH OTHER." (John 15:9-17)

In this essential passage, we learn what friendship with God through Christ is really about. We learn that God's great love comes forth to us through Christ, and that when we walk in the commandments of Christ, we remain in that love. What does this mean to us as friends of God through Christ and friends of one another? It means that obeying

God is where we find His love. The love of God is manifest in whatever it is that He has instructed of us to do, and therefore, we must understand His instructions to us. When we walk as God calls us to walk, we find ourselves in a place where we are free and able to know just how to love others. There's no question about what it looks like: we learn how to become friends with other people. When we are friends of God, we are able to embrace His words to us, and we are able to become the friends of other as we love them, too.

Years ago, I interviewed a pastor from a denomination I will admit I didn't know very much about back then. When I asked about evangelism efforts within the group, he said something to me that has stuck with me all these years: "We need to get out there and be other people's friends." I didn't expect that answer; I just assumed he would probably say something about going door-to-door or handing out tracts on the sidewalk. He didn't explain to me what he meant or how we were to do that, but I now understand he was referring to these Scriptures that instruct us to be friendly with other people. If we are truly in God, our friendship with Him should change our perspective and change the way we treat other people. This starting point is our friendship with God, and the result is our love, a sibling-like love, among those of us who are in the church.

YOU SEE, HIS FAITH AND HIS ACTIONS WORKED TOGETHER. HIS ACTIONS MADE HIS FAITH COMPLETE. AND SO IT HAPPENED JUST AS THE

SCRIPTURES SAY: "ABRAHAM BELIEVED GOD, AND GOD COUNTED HIM AS RIGHTEOUS BECAUSE OF HIS FAITH." HE WAS EVEN CALLED THE FRIEND OF GOD. SO YOU SEE, WE ARE SHOWN TO BE RIGHT WITH GOD BY WHAT WE DO, NOT BY FAITH ALONE. (James 2:22-24)

DON'T YOU REALIZE THAT FRIENDSHIP WITH THE WORLD MAKES YOU AN ENEMY OF GOD? I SAY IT AGAIN: IF YOU WANT TO BE A FRIEND OF THE WORLD, YOU MAKE YOURSELF AN ENEMY OF GOD. (James 4:4)

KEEP ON LOVING EACH OTHER AS BROTHERS AND SISTERS. (Hebrews 13:1)

We are the friends of God because our faith has demanded we become acquainted with and obedient to adopting an outlook in our lives that reflects love. The world doesn't reflect love – the world reflects selfishness, isolation, and distrust of others. Whenever we align ourselves to set forth with God, it changes our relationship with worldly systems and values. Friendship with God transforms the way we view the world; the way we view others; whether we view a stranger as a potential friend or an enemy; and if the quality of our relationship changes the way we interact with others.

This is the reason why God calls us friends and why we are to be friends. So many Christians think they will change the world with their beliefs or values, but that's not ultimately what brings about change. Our beliefs and values should change us, and in changing us, they should change the way we are with others (and as people, in general). The change we seek starts with us; with our own heart condition as we approach other people; and how we see them reflects in how we behave toward them. I've heard it said that even though we are all the children of God, some of us aren't aware of that fact yet. It's our job to bring forth this revelation in brotherly love, knowing a time will come when everyone will recognize the Lordship of Christ and we shall be transformed. While we await this time, let's be the transformation we seek, right now, today, in each and every possible way.

So, find your friends and spend time with them. Pray for your friends and with your friends. Don't be afraid to talk to your friends and inspire honest communication. Listen to them as much as you expect them to hear you. Start Bible studies with your Christian friends. Call up your friends and see how they are doing. Inspire brotherly love. Inspire friendship. It can – and will – change the world.

Reflections

- How is friendship a combination of all the different forms of love discussed thus far?

- How does friendship teach us about the difference between love and like?

- Why are friends important to our development as both social creatures and as believers?

- What do we do when friendship doesn't go as planned?

- What does it mean to be the friends of God through Christ?

Chapter Five

DIVINE LOVE (*AGAPE*)

> ### Agape[1]
> ἀγάπη, ης, ἡ, agape {ag-ah'-pay}
>
> **Meanings:**
> - love
> - affection
> - good will
> - love
> - benevolence
> - love feasts

OUR study in love has moved through several different phases to bring us to the place of divine love, or studying the most profound love possible: the love of God. It comes to us and then moves through us, changing how we feel about, view, and interact with others. It opens us up to the world, much as friendship does, but with a divine outlook, rather than an earthly one. While every person on earth can love people through attraction, friendship, as family members, and even through a sense of kindness, not everyone can look out on the world and view others with the same heart and intent that is rooted in God's love for them.

This is a special opportunity that is reserved for those who believe in God and come to know Him in a way that changes everything, from faith to life, realizing who we are and Who He is, with the power to transform the entire world. It is why we preach the Gospel; it is why we talk about Christ, it is why we embrace the love of God, it is why we want to tell everyone about His goodness and grace. The love of God provides so much insight and richness to our lives; we just can't keep it to ourselves.

By saving the best for last, we are concluding our look at the different words we translate as "love" with God's love, a fullness and expressiveness toward humankind: it teaches us so much about Him, who wouldn't want to run to the God we believe in and experience in our own lives? The sad truth is many haven't come to a place where they recognize God's love in their lives for what it is, and in missing it, they go looking for that sense of satisfaction and completion somewhere else. If we study more about the love of God in our lives, we will better recognize it for ourselves and show others where it is for them, as well. So here we will dive into this love that changes us from the inside out, making us new and taking us to new places, all thanks to God's intervention in our lives.

Properly defining agape

Agape is often defined as love in English, sometimes as charity or benevolence, but always as a higher form of love than mere attraction, interest, or even just friendship. As we can see from the definitions, it is associated with a sense of love that aspires for the highest good, the greatest aspirations possible, the best that anyone can have or offer. It gives unselfishly with good intentions, and no negative motives or after effects. For this reason, *agape* is really something beyond anything we can properly imagine or fathom with the natural mind. It doesn't make sense, doesn't sound logical, and recalls so many questions as to how something can be so pure, so amazing, and so incredible. Our answer is simple: it is because it is from God. That's what makes *agape* love so amazing and so perfect.

The principle of divine love

Whenever we hear about the love of God through Christ, sometimes the system and details don't make much sense to us now. Talks about ancient beliefs, sacrifice, blood offerings, and the general salvation process that existed in Biblical times might sound confusing, even barbaric. There are groups of people who have walked away from the faith, seeing it as a bloodthirsty system headed up by an evil, vengeful God that takes advantage of the innocent. This may very well be what this system sounds like by modern standards and in a modern ear, but that's not the message that was to be conveyed (which is why we, as Christians, must always strive for context and understanding). Even if people hear the story in this manner, they can't deny sin still exists, which makes it even more complicated to understand without background or context.

In the ancient world, blood was seen as the source of life, the life factor, the life facilitator. Because sin entered the world, it was seen as necessary for that life source, factor, facilitator to be offered in order to cover death with life. This might sound odd, but it was a statement that life had the power to overcome anything, even sin, even death. By offering various sacrifices (especially those that related to blood) we are able to see the promise of Christ's work to overcome sin from the earliest of times.

When we recognize the different sin offerings functioned by the simple concept that sin and death had to be conquered by the power of life is much more relatable and easier to understand in modern times than trying to sort through the specifics on different offerings (at least it is for the sake of this book). I think reading and studying the different offerings of the Old Testament is an awesome work to undertake, but the bottom line of every single offering is the principle of combatting death with life. As we talked about sin missing the mark God has set for us earlier, there had to be a way that we could overcome such actions and wrongdoing that has become part of human nature. This way was made for us through Jesus Christ, Who offered Himself as the sacrifice for all our sins.

"FOR THIS IS HOW GOD LOVED THE WORLD: HE GAVE HIS ONE AND ONLY SON, SO THAT EVERYONE WHO BELIEVES IN HIM WILL NOT PERISH BUT HAVE ETERNAL LIFE. GOD SENT HIS SON INTO THE WORLD NOT TO JUDGE THE WORLD, BUT TO SAVE THE WORLD THROUGH HIM.

"THERE IS NO JUDGMENT AGAINST ANYONE WHO BELIEVES IN HIM. BUT ANYONE WHO DOES NOT BELIEVE IN HIM HAS ALREADY BEEN JUDGED FOR NOT BELIEVING IN GOD'S ONE AND ONLY SON. AND THE JUDGMENT IS BASED ON THIS FACT: GOD'S LIGHT CAME INTO THE WORLD, BUT PEOPLE LOVED THE DARKNESS MORE THAN THE LIGHT, FOR THEIR ACTIONS WERE EVIL. ALL WHO DO EVIL HATE THE LIGHT AND REFUSE TO GO NEAR IT FOR FEAR THEIR SINS WILL BE EXPOSED. BUT THOSE WHO DO WHAT IS RIGHT COME TO THE LIGHT SO OTHERS CAN SEE THAT THEY ARE DOING WHAT GOD WANTS." (John 3:16-21)

Jesus didn't offer Himself for our sins because God is bloodthirsty and wicked. He did it out of that same love God has for each and every one of us, because it was His heart and desire that we would find our way back to God directly, breaking through sin and giving us the full opportunity to find union with God's love for ourselves. Everything about Jesus was life: He came from the Father in heaven to us on earth, He stood as the light, or guiding way, to the world, and He was willing to lay down His life to make a way for life. Christ's actions overcame sin and death, destroying their power, because He was, in

Himself, the way, the truth, and the life. It was so powerful, in fact, that He rose again from the dead three days after His death. Death couldn't hold back life. Even as a sacrifice for our sins, even by dying, death still couldn't hold Him!

This is the power of God's love at work. God knew what had to be done, and it was done through His Son. It is so important to hear the passage of John 3:16-21 for real this time in the context of love, rather than just something popular and passing for evangelism class. God so loved the world that He was willing to do this, all out of love! It wasn't out of judgment, nor hate, nor analyzing, nor feeling any which way about the world, nor ignoring the world, nor loving the world from a distance, nor loving the world but not in love with the world, nor feeling some kind of way about the world, nor liking the world but not loving it...God loved the world! That is a message that should cause us to shout from here through eternity. Christ was willing to die for our sins out of love for us! That sacrifice, that willingness to lay down for others, despite us, is what makes this the greatest love story of all time. Despite our faults and failings, despite all those times we missed the mark of sin and alienated ourselves, God still made a way of life over death with the ability to empower and overcome. He didn't have to do it, but He did, and for that, we find love.

This teaches us all we need to know about divine love: it is the great overcomer that seeks the highest good, the encouragement and ability to overcome death with life, and being willing to sacrifice oneself so others can also live. It's something we receive and then we live, not necessarily dying for everyone we know, but in being willing to lay down our flesh, our habits, and everything about us that leads to death so that we can bring others to this powerful life, the love of God manifesting and living in us.

God is love

The concept that God is love wasn't seen until New Testament times. The reason for this is simple: the first-century believers were so moved by the love of God present in Christ's sacrifice for their sins that this revealed a whole side to God that seldom before had anyone experienced in its full form. We can see the incredible love God had for His people in the Old Testament, as that love manifested time and time again when God continually reached out to a people that often rejected Him. Yet the overwhelming promise of life in Christ, realizing that God's Son was the sacrifice for our sins, made the early church adopt an entirely new outlook on God's love than they ever had seen before. It challenged them, not just to receive God's love for themselves, but to love others in a different way than just as mere acquaintances. The early church challenged us to love everyone we encounter – with the love of God.

DEAR FRIENDS, LET US CONTINUE TO LOVE ONE ANOTHER, FOR LOVE COMES FROM GOD. ANYONE WHO LOVES IS A CHILD OF GOD AND KNOWS GOD.

Dr. Lee Ann B. Marino, Ph.D., D.Min., D.D.

But anyone who does not love does not know God, for God is love.

God showed how much He loved us by sending His one and only Son into the world so that we might have eternal life through Him. This is real love—not that we loved God, but that He loved us and sent His Son as a sacrifice to take away our sins.

Dear friends, since God loved us that much, we surely ought to love each other. No one has ever seen God. But if we love each other, God lives in us, and his love is brought to full expression in us.

And God has given us His Spirit as proof that we live in Him and He in us. Furthermore, we have seen with our own eyes and now testify that the Father sent His Son to be the Savior of the world. All who declare that Jesus is the Son of God have God living in them, and they live in God. We know how much God loves us, and we have put our trust in his love.

God is love, and all who live in love live in God, and God lives in them. And as we live in God, our love grows more perfect. So we will not be afraid on the day of judgment, but we can face Him with confidence because we live like Jesus here in this world.

Such love has no fear, because perfect love expels all fear. If we are afraid, it is

FOR FEAR OF PUNISHMENT, AND THIS SHOWS THAT WE HAVE NOT FULLY EXPERIENCED HIS PERFECT LOVE. WE LOVE EACH OTHER BECAUSE HE LOVED US FIRST.

IF SOMEONE SAYS, "I LOVE GOD," BUT HATES A FELLOW BELIEVER, THAT PERSON IS A LIAR; FOR IF WE DON'T LOVE PEOPLE WE CAN SEE, HOW CAN WE LOVE GOD, WHOM WE CANNOT SEE? AND HE HAS GIVEN US THIS COMMAND: THOSE WHO LOVE GOD MUST ALSO LOVE THEIR FELLOW BELIEVERS. (1 John 4:7-21)

If we claim to know God, then we must express our union with God by loving other people. We are challenged to love others with the highest good, seeking exactly what we would desire for ourselves (outfitted with godly perspective and vision) for every person we meet. We are able to love others because the Spirit of God lives within us, therefore we know the way we can go because we are divinely directed, led of life Himself, and we are living surrounded by the love of God. It is a good love; a love we can trust, one that does not let us down, and lifts us up to a place where we are safe, without fear, and most importantly, without hate.

It's that last point where many often trip up because hate is a part of the flesh, a part of this world, a consequence of alienation and isolation. We can express hate for others and conveniently convince ourselves that it's something else: principle, belief, conviction, ideas, self-preservation, or self-defense. This happens all the time and is so common, we have entire groups of people who cheer on hatred and embitterment as some sort of personal crusade, as a good thing, a way of identifying together and supporting values and morals. The reality, however, is that it doesn't matter why you hate your neighbor, because hating someone else is hate, even if you don't call it such. If you don't stand beside someone else and desire for them what you would desire for yourself – the highest good imaginable manifest in their lives – then you don't love them. You can try and spin it any way you want – claiming to hate sin but love sinners, believing in the Bible, upholding morality, believing in traditional values – but if your motive is to promote yourself above them, you do not really love them.

There's no doubt that love and the concept of love is highly distorted in our world. Love doesn't mean giving everyone their own way all the time. It doesn't mean we become floormats and just let people railroad us. It also doesn't mean that everything people do is right or that we must agree with what they do. What it does mean is that we step back and as a people set apart to do the work of God in this world, we don't judge others. We let God stand as judge and we stand willing to work with others and to pray for them, to encourage them, to guide as we are so called and led to do, and most of all, set a good example for them in what it looks like to be loved by God. We can show forth the transformation that the love of God has had upon us and extend that to others in everything we do.

God is love because God is the ultimate, foundational source of love. All love comes from God and connects us to Him. The full expression of His love is manifest in us not when we have great experiences or miracles, but when we love one another. This is not to say miracles aren't great and great spiritual experiences aren't important, but that if we want to see the fullness of God's love manifest within us and within our spiritual lives, we need to see His love bring about a change. Our behavior changes when we are loved by God, receiving and accepting that love, and living it out. That is what shows Him – and others – that we have been sincerely changed by love.

Some translations of the Bible translate *agape* as "charity," which has led some to believe that the love of God is a handout or a form of pity, of sorts. It is translated that way not because God thinks we are pitiful (if you look at sin we often are, but that's another matter), but because God's love is freely given to us without cost. We could never pay enough, do enough, or be enough to earn that love – it is just there, just given to us because it is Who God is. A love like this is hard to fathom if we use human measure, which is why it is so often misunderstood and misaligned by the world. Who can ever fathom such a powerful love with a human mind? Fathom it or not, it does exist!

What divine love looks like

1 Corinthians 13:4-8 is often read at weddings, which has led many to believe that it is an expression of marital love. While there's nothing wrong with encouraging the presence and experience of *agape* love in

marriage, that's not the exclusive context of such spiritual love. *Agape* love is something that's not just for marriage; it is for everyone. In us, it is the very product – a fruit, if you will – of what God has done and how the love of God has changed us.

IF I COULD SPEAK ALL THE LANGUAGES OF EARTH AND OF ANGELS, BUT DIDN'T LOVE OTHERS, I WOULD ONLY BE A NOISY GONG OR A CLANGING CYMBAL. IF I HAD THE GIFT OF PROPHECY, AND IF I UNDERSTOOD ALL OF GOD'S SECRET PLANS AND POSSESSED ALL KNOWLEDGE, AND IF I HAD SUCH FAITH THAT I COULD MOVE MOUNTAINS, BUT DIDN'T LOVE OTHERS, I WOULD BE NOTHING. IF I GAVE EVERYTHING I HAVE TO THE POOR AND EVEN SACRIFICED MY BODY, I COULD BOAST ABOUT IT; BUT IF I DIDN'T LOVE OTHERS, I WOULD HAVE GAINED NOTHING.

LOVE IS PATIENT AND KIND. LOVE IS NOT JEALOUS OR BOASTFUL OR PROUD OR RUDE. IT DOES NOT DEMAND ITS OWN WAY. IT IS NOT IRRITABLE, AND IT KEEPS NO RECORD OF BEING WRONGED. IT DOES NOT REJOICE ABOUT INJUSTICE BUT REJOICES WHENEVER THE TRUTH WINS OUT. LOVE NEVER GIVES UP, NEVER LOSES FAITH, IS ALWAYS HOPEFUL, AND ENDURES THROUGH EVERY CIRCUMSTANCE.

PROPHECY AND SPEAKING IN UNKNOWN LANGUAGES AND SPECIAL KNOWLEDGE WILL BECOME USELESS. BUT LOVE WILL LAST FOREVER! NOW OUR KNOWLEDGE IS PARTIAL AND INCOMPLETE, AND EVEN THE GIFT OF PROPHECY REVEALS ONLY PART OF THE WHOLE PICTURE!

BUT WHEN THE TIME OF PERFECTION COMES, THESE PARTIAL THINGS WILL BECOME USELESS.

WHEN I WAS A CHILD, I SPOKE AND THOUGHT AND REASONED AS A CHILD. BUT WHEN I GREW UP, I PUT AWAY CHILDISH THINGS. NOW WE SEE THINGS IMPERFECTLY, LIKE PUZZLING REFLECTIONS IN A MIRROR, BUT THEN WE WILL SEE EVERYTHING WITH PERFECT CLARITY. ALL THAT I KNOW NOW IS PARTIAL AND INCOMPLETE, BUT THEN I WILL KNOW EVERYTHING COMPLETELY, JUST AS GOD NOW KNOWS ME COMPLETELY.

THREE THINGS WILL LAST FOREVER—FAITH, HOPE, AND LOVE—AND THE GREATEST OF THESE IS LOVE. (1 Corinthians 13:1-13)

I've started our look at what divine love looks like with the first verse of 1 Corinthians 13, stretching all the way to verse 13. There is a reason for this: we tend to isolate about four verses from this chapter without reading the entirety in context. There are some very key things in the entire chapter that help us to see the reality of how divine love works for us and through us.

The first thing we should recognize about divine love is that without it we are nothing. We can be the first ones in line to make a great show of spiritual displays, even make grand gestures toward others, but if we do not have love, it doesn't mean much. We can do all the right things (as we discussed in one of our earlier chapters), say all the right things, look the part, and seemingly appear like we've got it all together, only to be...absolutely nothing. This may sound harsh, even unfair, but the Scriptures tell us this because if we lack God in our lives, we are missing something very central to the purpose of our existence. The primary reason why we exist – before all other reasons – is to know and experience God. Those who don't come to know God for themselves might have some encounters with love, they might even feel a sense or presence at some times, but when it comes to discovering where – and Who – that love leads us, knowing God is the only way to fully embrace His love so it makes a lasting change in our lives. Remember, what we do in love must stem from something; it must come from a foundational point! It is our purpose that the love we express to others will lead them back to the Originator of that love. Therefore, we can't operate in true divine love, and it divide from or exist separate from God.

That means that *agape* love is not always love as we might understand it in a human sense. It's not rational within our minds, because it comes from a God Who loves us beyond all reason and gives us an entire lifetime to get ourselves right and straight from a heavenly perspective. So to say that love is patient and kind tells us about the attributes of God toward us as much as it says how we interact when we are walking in His love. We recognize we serve a God Who is patient (long-suffering) and showers us in His kindness. It's not about what we deserve, but all about Who He is, because those things are Him.

The reverse of this is if we've received it, we should be able to give it. Such attributes, such love change us. We should see ourselves more patient and kinder toward others. It doesn't mean we get it right all the time, but it should be notable that we can see a before and after transformation at some point in our walk with God. God stands as our example of how to treat other people, not as a demanding requirement, but by showing us the way to true and lasting results.

We then go on to see what love is by contrasting it with what it is not. Love is not jealous, it's not proud, it's not boastful. This means that love isn't selfish. When we are jealous, we want to keep something to ourselves or all for ourselves. In pride, we esteem ourselves as better than and more highly than others. In boasting, we brag about how great we feel we are (whether others agree with us, or not). Such behaviors send loud and clear messages about how we feel about ourselves and how we feel about others, even if that's not the message we intend to convey. Behaving in these ways is contrary to love because it keeps us from extending patience and kindness to others. Likewise, love doesn't demand its own way, isn't irritable, and doesn't keep track of wrongs. In other words, love isn't all about oneself. Just as God doesn't demand of us (He guides, He advises, He instructs but still leaves us free to make our own choice if we decide to go another way), neither act in irritation with us, nor failing to forgive us as we need. God rejoices when good things happen to us, not bad. The truth winning out in our lives (accepting truth in each and every situation) is a source of joy for Him, not threat or competition. He never gives up on us or loses faith in us, always believes in hope, and endures with us.

Anyone who has lived to adulthood recognizes these are pretty difficult things for us to embody in our interactions with others. That's the point; we can't accomplish them with anyone on our own. No amount of positive visualization, affirmations, confessions, or cheerleading is going to help us to love other people in a transformative way. If we want to receive the results of divine love, we must receive the love of God. If want to give the results of divine love, we must make the effort to allow that love to do its full work within us.

1 Corinthians 13:11-13 is not criticizing spiritual gifts or their work in one's life. It was the Apostle Paul Himself who talked extensively about such gifts in 1 Corinthians 12. His goal wasn't to cause confusion, but to remind all of us that no matter how amazingly spiritual we may regard ourselves to be, God knows us and knows the power by which we operate. Spiritual signs can be imitated or mocked, but only the true power of God can work love within us. One day, the spiritual gifts we love and rest ourselves upon will fade away. This day has not yet come, but when Christ as love incarnate returns to us, we will recognize things perfectly and not need the various expressions we require now to be reminded of His presence. Maturity is required to walk in true love, and as God knows us, when we come to a mature place, we know God. This leads to more signs of love in our lives, which as we know, shall last into

eternity.

Love is here to prepare us for eternal things in a way that nothing else this side of heaven can provide. It requires us to act differently, to straighten up and mature, and to become more than we ever thought possible. Love does the impossible within us and through us, and that means whenever we come to interact with love, we are becoming the very person God desires us to be. God is love, as our Father God is our Originator, and that means true love comes from only one source – God.

God first

We all love to go to church and throw our hands up in the air, singing pretty songs that proclaim how "God is first" in our lives. It makes us feel good, maybe even instilling a sense of pride within about how good we are to make God our priority. Then we leave that church and chaos begins. We have trouble on our job. We have issues in our families. We don't get along with other people. We skip our prayer, devotional, or Scripture study time. We might even miss more church services than we attend, but we are quick to say that "God is first." Is He? If we start to challenge that notion, we must become defensive, but there are realities to consider. God is not first in your life because you wear T-shirts with Bible verses on them or avoid bad language in movies. God being first in your life indicates a specific set of priorities.

The truth is that for most people, God is not their first priority; they are. Nobody is honest enough to admit this, however. It'll manifest in the flurry of different components that make up and create one's life and will disguise itself as necessary tasks that create the building blocks to that life and its responsibility. These tasks have one united component: they are all there with the intended goal of producing one's visions and ideals, and those ideals and concepts may have nothing to do with the aspiration or goal of putting God first. They are often just things people think they want to accomplish or need to have in their lives. Those things become perceived as needs or necessities, and they are what many pursue, while putting the intents and desires of God on the back burner.

They may sound like admirable things – family, career, new cars, bigger house, better appliances, established finances – but if God isn't at the very base of our aspirations, no matter how good or admirable they may be, they aren't the things we should aim to seek.

SEEK THE KINGDOM OF GOD ABOVE ALL ELSE, AND LIVE RIGHTEOUSLY, AND HE WILL GIVE YOU EVERYTHING YOU NEED. (Matthew 6:33)

How do we seek the Kingdom of God above all else? We seek the King that leads it!

ONE OF THE TEACHERS OF RELIGIOUS LAW WAS STANDING THERE LISTENING TO THE DEBATE. HE REALIZED THAT JESUS HAD ANSWERED WELL, SO HE ASKED, "OF ALL THE COMMANDMENTS, WHICH IS THE MOST IMPORTANT?"

Jesus replied, "The most important commandment is this: 'Listen, O Israel! The Lord our God is the one and only Lord. And you must love the Lord your God with all your heart, all your soul, all your mind, and all your strength.' The second is equally important: 'Love your neighbor as yourself.' No other commandment is greater than these."

The teacher of religious law replied, "Well said, Teacher. You have spoken the truth by saying that there is only one God and no other. And I know it is important to love Him with all my heart and all my understanding and all my strength, and to love my neighbor as myself. This is more important than to offer all of the burnt offerings and sacrifices required in the law."

Realizing how much the man understood, Jesus said to him, "You are not far from the Kingdom of God." And after that, no one dared to ask Him any more questions. (Mark 12:28-34)

It would stand to reason that those teachers of religious law who were always testing Jesus desired to vindicate themselves by trapping Him in questions and conundrums they thought difficult to answer. They thought they knew better than everyone else, so they would take His understanding of Scripture to the ultimate test. The Jews recognized hundreds of commands – over six hundred in total – so the question posed to Jesus was:

Which one was most important? By asking this, he was asking Jesus to pick and choose between them. If one was more important than the other, then surely breaking certain ones was more acceptable than breaking others. It was a test because it existed to pit different commandments against each other, thus vindicating the leaders who broke commandments at their convenience while holding others to their literal interpretation.

This makes Jesus' answer – to pay attention, listen and acknowledge God is the only true God and that you are to love God with all your heart, soul, mind, and strength – very, very important. It is through this love that we have for God that we learn about Him and more of interaction with Him. Those we love we spend time with, and God is no different. It should be the posture of every acclaimed believer to devote and spend that time getting to know God. As we know Him, we put Him and His will first in our lives because we become better acquainted with what that will looks like. We will understand greater why He calls us to certain things, and as we answer, we will trust Him more and more.

We are to love God first. Period. That's before our own wants and needs, before our families, before our personal desires and aspirations, and before all those things we can live without. That's what Jesus was saying. His answer was so startling, in fact, that the teacher of the law had no response but to agree with Christ's words. Instead of contradicting the Scriptures, Christ showed their inherent unity. If we put God first, we will not set ourselves against anything He lays out for us.

But wait – what about that second commandment, that "love your neighbor" part? What does that have to do with anything? Everything!

Who is my neighbor?

The question about how we love our neighbor as ourselves has haunted Christians for centuries. Are we supposed to just love other Christians? Is the command to love a neighbor about every single person we encounter? Is it just about our literal neighbors, the people who live next door? Is it about our neighboring countries? Who exactly is my neighbor?

ONE DAY AN EXPERT IN RELIGIOUS LAW STOOD UP TO TEST JESUS BY ASKING HIM THIS QUESTION: "TEACHER, WHAT SHOULD I DO TO INHERIT ETERNAL LIFE?"

JESUS REPLIED, "WHAT DOES THE LAW OF MOSES SAY? HOW DO YOU READ IT?"

THE MAN ANSWERED, "'YOU MUST LOVE THE LORD YOUR GOD WITH ALL YOUR HEART, ALL YOUR SOUL, ALL YOUR STRENGTH, AND ALL YOUR MIND.' AND, 'LOVE YOUR NEIGHBOR AS YOURSELF.'"

"RIGHT!" JESUS TOLD HIM. "DO THIS AND YOU WILL LIVE!"

The man wanted to justify his actions, so he asked Jesus, "And who is my neighbor?"

Jesus replied with a story: "A Jewish man was traveling from Jerusalem down to Jericho, and he was attacked by bandits. They stripped him of his clothes, beat him up, and left him half dead beside the road.

"By chance a priest came along. But when he saw the man lying there, he crossed to the other side of the road and passed him by. A Temple assistant walked over and looked at him lying there, but he also passed by on the other side.

"Then a despised Samaritan came along, and when he saw the man, he felt compassion for him. Going over to him, the Samaritan soothed his wounds with olive oil and wine and bandaged them. Then he put the man on his own donkey and took him to an inn, where he took care of him. The next day he handed the innkeeper two silver coins, telling him, 'Take care of this man. If his bill runs higher than this, I'll pay you the next time I'm here.'

"Now which of these three would you say was a neighbor to the man who was attacked by bandits?" Jesus asked.

The man replied, "The one who showed him mercy."

Then Jesus said, "Yes, now go and do the same." (Luke 10:25-37)

Let's understand Jesus' words to end any debate on who exactly we are to love as our "neighbor." Jesus' example of a righteous Samaritan in the face of Jewish priests and temple assistants who behaved in a manner that was unrighteous was most convicting and timely for the first century. It's relevant for us, today, as well, but we have to be willing to hear it for ourselves to understand just how important it is today.

In Jesus' day, the Jews and the Samaritans absolutely despised each other. The Jews looked down on the Samaritans as pagan idolaters who took part of the law and mixed it with pagan customs and beliefs. This is exactly what happened in history, as the Samaritans came into existence when pagan idolaters were more or less (emphasize less) evangelized by unsuccessful missionary attempts handled by priests during Old Testament times. The result was an intermingling of belief systems, with the Samaritans claiming to be the true religion of the Israelites prior to the Babylonian captivity. This conflict led Jews and Samaritans to hold particular distain and hatred for each other, as the Jews didn't believe the Samaritans were legitimate and the Samaritans didn't believe the Jews were legitimate. As close neighbors, Samaritans and Jews intolerably co-existed, refusing to have anything to do with the other.

Jesus' story, however, proves that true love of our neighbor isn't dependent on what our neighbor might believe. It was the Samaritan who helped the Jewish man who was attacked, robbed, and beaten, and not his own Jewish brethren. Those who should have been responsible and interested in his care were not; they were too concerned about looking right, being in the right place at the right time, and avoiding any and all contact with the injured man. It was the Samaritan – the one who was technically forbidden to interact with the Jews – who stepped up to help this man, care for him, assume financial responsibility, and ultimately become an agent of care and compassion in a difficult situation.

So who is your neighbor? Your neighbor is anyone and everyone, from the person standing next to you to the next person you meet who is in need and you are reasonably able to help them. Our neighbor is anyone, whether they are like us, and especially if they are different from us. This command to love our neighbor as ourselves expresses the ultimate in divine love and opens it up for others to experience the product of our close relationship with God.

Love and the narrow way

We have all heard Christianity spoken of as a "narrow way." Such is often spoken to indicate that the regulations and confines of Christianity are constricting, and the majority won't follow them unto the end of eternal salvation. There is some truth in this, but many who advocate such logic are endorsing faith by works. They are saying that in order to be saved, you must follow many arbitrary rules that are almost never Biblical or taken largely out of Scriptural context. There's a lot of reasons why the attitude many have behind the saying don't hold up, but there is an important reason why many often don't make it through Christianity in the way they might hope or anticipate. That reason is because love is a difficult path to follow, far harder than hate, and far more trying than any rule or regulation we can try to live by without proper understanding. It's not to say we can live any way we so please in Christianity or that groups shouldn't have rules; but it is to say that the ultimate goal of any rule or any regulation should be to force us to look at and examine just where love is in our lives and where it can be better.

"YOU HAVE HEARD THE LAW THAT SAYS, 'LOVE YOUR NEIGHBOR' AND HATE YOUR ENEMY. BUT I SAY, LOVE YOUR ENEMIES! PRAY FOR THOSE WHO PERSECUTE YOU! IN THAT WAY, YOU WILL BE ACTING AS TRUE CHILDREN OF YOUR FATHER IN HEAVEN. FOR HE GIVES HIS SUNLIGHT TO BOTH THE EVIL AND THE GOOD, AND HE SENDS RAIN ON THE JUST AND THE UNJUST ALIKE. IF YOU LOVE ONLY THOSE WHO LOVE YOU, WHAT REWARD IS THERE FOR THAT? EVEN CORRUPT TAX COLLECTORS DO THAT MUCH. IF YOU ARE KIND ONLY TO YOUR FRIENDS, HOW ARE YOU DIFFERENT FROM ANYONE ELSE? EVEN PAGANS DO THAT." (Matthew 5:43-47)

To put it simply, in love, we must examine ourselves. Wherever we aren't measuring up, we must change.

What makes this hard is the fact that we just don't always like the people we meet or deal within our lives. Being someone's preferred preference or the kind of person one might "like" to be friends with is different from the spiritual discipline of loving someone unto *agape*. In *agape*, we earnestly seek and believe for others what we would seek for ourselves. This is radically unlike wanting to hang out with someone and liking them as a person. In *agape*, we love others because it kills the flesh within us that wants to put ourselves first. God does not command us to like everyone; He commands us to love them.

That makes this work of love very, very hard...but we can do all things through Christ, even love God, and love others.

Everyone loves those they like. It's easy to love those who reflect the best we see in ourselves and who make us feel comfortable and assured as we are. It's a lot harder to embrace the challenge of loving our enemies because they reveal things within us that still need to change. Our enemies bring out our tempers, our feelings of inadequacy, our flaws and imperfections, and sometimes, in the face of our enemies we see things we used to be or still are if we refuse to change and transform. Enemies bring us face-to-face with the hard work that love does within us. It's not that we hate in them what they remind us about ourselves, but our flesh resists our response to change toward them.

The hard truth remains, however: even those who aren't believers love those who love them back. It doesn't cost us nor take us as much to do that. Loving our enemies? Loving those who have wronged us? Loving those who have shown us what not to do in life? It doesn't mean cozying up to them and becoming their best friend. In fact, we might never see or hear from them ever again. It means we want for them the highest good of what we want for ourselves. It is only then that we turn them over to God, in full, and allow God to work in their lives to reach them, no matter how He desires to do so. He increases, we decrease, and we stop interfering in the process to be right or to get our own retribution, instead stepping aside to let God be God in every possible way.

It would appear that we have a great work to accomplish through this powerful love of God, the love that has the power to soften the hardest sinner and empower the weakest person. We are here to love everyone, no matter who they might be, despite what criticism we may have of them. God doesn't ask that we understand everything, but that we are willing to trust Him enough to let His love infill, overflow, and change everything we touch – from our friends to our enemies. Do you trust Him enough to let love change your life – but first to change you?

Reflections

- How does divine love relate to eternal life?

- How do we come to understand and see that God is love?

- What does divine love look like?

- What are the two most important commandments, and why are they relevant to love?

- How are love and the narrow way of Christianity related?

Conclusion

CONNECTED BY LOVE

THE nature of love is something that is often hard to describe. We can recognize it when we feel it, we know when we do not feel it, and it can change everything it touches. It's a part of life; a part of us; a part of our eternity, because it is our eternity. It is one of a handful of things that will transfer from this life into the next, for one simple reason: God is love, and God will be with us no matter what happens or where we go. When the world as we know it is different and life is quite different, love will remain a central (if not the central) part of our experience.

Every time we experience love we are experiencing a part of the wholeness of God. God loves us in all ways, all at once, and brings us to a new and profound realization of Who He is and who we are. So often, we try to fix ourselves using human methods and ideas. We'll try to puff ourselves up and make ourselves feel better by putting others down or exalting ourselves above where we should be or where it is wise for us to be, but we always feel like we wind up short. Our best attempts sometimes puff us for a bit, but at the end of many days, we still feel broken and lost, wishing and hoping for a love that transcends our flaws.

Then there are those who are uncertain of how to love others rightly and balanced, always fighting the temptation to put themselves above everyone else. It's fine to love ourselves (the Scriptures themselves say we love our neighbor as ourselves), but the problem is that loving ourselves exclusively means we leave love of others out of the equation. Love is meant to be shared and experienced, because it is an essential part of life. Any time we expect to receive and not give, we aren't understanding, nor properly walking in love. Love recognizes it's not all about us, all the time, and in loving others, we not only return God's love, but we also experience it in a whole new way.

Love is a point of connection. In this life there are many things we might have in common with other people, but only love stands to connect us for life: this life and life to come. It connects us with eternity, giving us a taste and a promise of all that is to come and reveal itself to us through God's goodness when our world changes. Our world will, one day, change. One day, everything we aspire to as pertains to this life – our monetary system, our worldly goals, the fake friends and connections, the problems we experience, our intense trials and griefs – will all pass away.

This world as we understand it will be no more, and we will experience a union with God and one another that can only be described as love. It will be built on powerful faith, as we will see the Perfect – Jesus – with us, in our midst, and we will no longer find ourselves sad or unhappy. No longer will we struggle to love others, God, and ourselves. Instead, love will be our literal way of being.

It's great to talk about this coming time. It is definitely something we should seek to learn about. It's something to think about and realize just how great it will be. But love is our connection between "then" and "now." Our world might not be perfect, but we can connect in love with others, so we experience those moments that prepare us for what is to come. They may not be exactly the way it'll be, but they reveal, unveil, connect us with something that is beyond our comprehension and understanding for the time being. We walk in it and feel it and know it's real because if we can see it right now, through our darkened, dim glass, we can only imagine just how amazing it will be in time to come.

Love is our ultimate connection between God, others, and us. It is also our amazing preparer for things to come that we cannot yet fully see or know by anything but our faith. The more we walk in it, the more we will experience God and the fullness of life He has for us. What keeps you from walking in love in your life? From experiencing it, giving it, walking in it, receiving it, sharing it, and connecting through it? How can you come to know a deeper love of God? How can you feel His love better in your life? How can you give and receive love with others in a better way?

Embrace love. Pursue love. Choose love. Walk in love. It's the only hope for this world and the only thing that connects us while we await what is next. As people often say, love wins…it wins because love is, always and forever, of, from, and embodied in God.

References

Chapter 1

[1] *Strong's Exhaustive Concordance of the Bible*, #0157
[2] "Greek Words for Love." https://en.wikipedia.org/wiki/Greek_words_for_love. Accessed September 5, 2018.
[3] "Eros." https://en.wikipedia.org/wiki/Eros. Accessed September 5, 2018.

Chapter 2

[1] *Strong's Exhaustive Concordance of the Bible*, #5387
[2] Ibid.

Chapter 3

[1] *Strong's Exhaustive Concordance of the Bible*, #2617

Chapter 4

[1] *Strong's Exhaustive Concordance of the Bible*,

#7355
²Ibid., #5360

Chapter 5

¹*Strong's Exhaustive Concordance of the Bible*, #**26**

About The Author

DR. LEE ANN B. MARINO, PH.D., D.MIN., D.D.

DR. LEE ANN B. MARINO, PH.D., D.MIN., D.D. (she/her) is "everyone's favorite theologian" leading Gen X, Millennials, and Gen Z with expertise in leadership training, queer and feminist theology, general religion, and apostolic theology. She has served in ministry since 1998 and was ordained as a pastor in 2002 and an apostle in 2010. She founded what is now Sanctuary Apostolic Fellowship Empowerment (SAFE) Ministries in 2004. Under her ministry heading Dr. Marino is founder and Overseer of Sanctuary International Fellowship Tabernacle (SIFT) (the original home of National Coming Out Sunday) and The Sanctuary Network, and Chancellor of Apostolic Covenant Theological Seminary (ACTS).

Affectionately nicknamed "the Spitfire," Dr. Marino has spent over two decades as an "apostle, preacher, and teacher" (2 Timothy 1:11), exercising her personal mandate to become "all things to all people" (1 Corinthians 9:22). Her embrace of spiritual issues (both technical and intimate) has found its home among both seekers and believers, those who desire spiritual answers to today's issues.

Dr. Marino has preached throughout the United States, Puerto Rico, and Europe in hundreds of religious services and experiences throughout the years. A history maker in her own right, she has spent over two decades in advocacy, education, and work for and within minority spiritual communities (including African American, Hispanic, and LGBTQ+). She has also served as the first woman on all-male synods, councils, and panels, as well as the first preacher or speaker welcomed of a different race, sexual orientation, or identity among diverse communities. Today, Dr. Marino's work extends to over 150 countries as she hosts the popular *Kingdom Now* podcast, which is in the top 20 percentile of all podcasts worldwide. She is also the author of over 35 books and the popular Patheos column, *Leadership on Fire*. To date, she has had five bestselling titles within their subject matter: *Understanding Demonology, Spiritual Warfare, Healing, and Deliverance: A Manual for the Christian Minister*; *Ministry School Boot Camp: Training for Helps Ministries, Appointments, and Beyond*; *Discovering Intimacy: A Journey Through the Song of Solomon*; *Fruit of the Vine: Study and Commentary on the Fruit of the Spirit*; and *Ministering to LGBTQ+ (and Those Who Love Them): A Primer for Queer Theology* (and its accompanying workbook).

As a public icon and social media influencer, Dr. Marino advocates healthy body image (curvy/full-figured), representation as a demisexual/aromantic, and albinism awareness as a model. Known to those she works with, she is a spiritual mom, teacher, leader, professor, confidant, and friend. She continues to transform, receiving new teaching, revelation, and insight in this thing we call "ministry." Through years of spiritual growth and maturity, Dr. Marino stands as herself, here to present what God has given to her for any who have an ear to hear.

For more information, visit her website at kingdompowernow.org.

www.ingramcontent.com/pod-product-compliance
Lightning Source LLC
Chambersburg PA
CBHW051342040426
42453CB00007B/375